Planning and Implementing Electronic Records Management

A practical guide

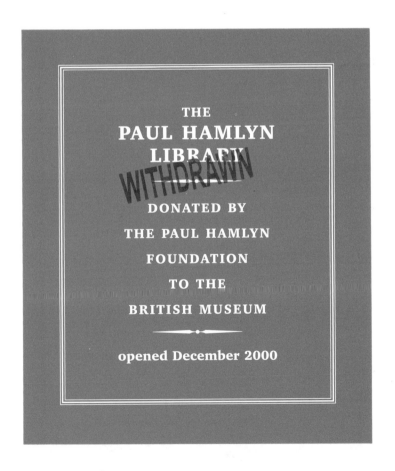

By the same author

Kelvin Smith *Freedom of Information: a practical guide to implementing the Act*, 2004, ISBN 978-1-85604-517-9

Planning and Implementing Electronic Records Management

A practical guide

Kelvin Smith

facet publishing

© Kelvin Smith 2007

Published by Facet Publishing
7 Ridgmount Street, London WC1E 7AE
www.facetpublishing.co.uk

Facet Publishing is wholly owned by CILIP: the Chartered Institute of Library and
Information Professionals.

Kelvin Smith has asserted his right under the Copyright, Designs and Patents Act,
1988, to be identified as author of this work.

British Library Cataloguing in Publication Data
A catalogue record for this book is available from the British Library.

ISBN 978-1-85604-615-2
First published 2007
Reprinted 2009

Typeset in 10/13pt Revival 565 and Nimbus Sans by Facet Publishing.
Printed and bound in Great Britain by the MPG. Books Group

Contents

Introduction

First of all I would like to emphasize that this book focuses very much on the practical aspects of the planning and implementation of electronic records management systems. It does not dwell on academic theory; while it puts the theory of the subject into context where necessary, explaining for example the role of authenticity, reliability and integrity of electronic records, its aim is to provide you with practical guidance that enables you to get on and do electronic records management.

The book is aimed at information managers in all organizations, in both public and private sectors. You may be records managers, archivists or even knowledge managers. Whatever area is your focus, the content of the following pages has been designed to meet that situation where your management board or executive team have just declared that 'we had better look at how we can manage our information more effectively and more efficiently' or 'let's go ahead and acquire an electronic records management system' - and you and your colleagues have been told to get on and do it. The layout follows a logical pattern and tries where possible to provide examples and pointers to further information, such as sample requirements and references to detailed toolkits. A glossary of frequently used terms appears in Chapter 2 (page 19).

The opening chapter describes the underlying principles of records management but for the most part the following pages presume that you have some grounding in the subject and that your organization has at least given the go-ahead to examine the feasibility of introducing electronic records management. It may even have made a firm commitment in that direction.

Software solutions to implement electronic records management are now so numerous and diverse that it would be impossible to provide guidance in the form of a detailed toolkit. To a large extent you will want the software to fit your business needs, not the other way round. You need to tell suppliers what you need, not let them tell you what you think you need. In this respect the requirements at the end of the chapters in Part 2 on design are necessarily a sample and set at a high level. Detailed requirements necessary for effective planning and implementation need to be developed according to individual organizational requirements. Implementing electronic records management is much more than implementing a piece of software. It is an activity, and issues such as business planning, change management and training have to be taken into account.

In maintaining its practical focus the book does not examine in great detail the many inter-related subjects such as intranets, websites and wikis. Before very long, however, these will probably form a package with electronic records management, and further theories and practices will be developed. Already we are seeing a great deal written about enterprise content management systems. This inter-relationship is examined briefly at the beginning of Chapter 4 (see page 57).

Before you plunge into the following pages, may I make a couple of important points? Firstly, it will take longer than you think to plan and implement an electronic records management system. About ten years ago it was suggested in the UK central government sector that it could be done in five years. We have learnt from experience. Think more of seven, eight or even nine years, if you are starting from scratch. Secondly, never forget that you can learn an awful lot from other peoples' experiences. Many people in many organizations have been through the process already and most have lived to tell the tale.

Acknowledgements

I have very many people and organizations to be thankful for in putting this book together. I hope the omissions from the following will not feel too aggrieved. The organizations to which I am grateful include:

The National Archives, where I have enjoyed working for the past forty years and, I hope, made a modest contribution to the mass of advice and guidance which it has produced. It has been quite sobering and revealing to re-visit some of those original publications.

The Joint Information Services Committee (JISC) which, through its records manager Steve Bailey, has done a tremendous amount of work on explaining the implementation of electronic records management in the higher education sector.

The National Archives of Australia which has in recent years distinguished itself by some very innovative thinking in records management and has pushed forward an active agenda for introducing electronic records management into the Australian government.

The Office of Government Commerce (OGC) whose guidance on procurement is second to none.

The Department of Health for permission to use their survey on the implementation of electronic records management.

The National Weights and Measures Laboratory for permission to use their appraisal report.

Records staff of English Nature (now part of Natural England) for being able to draw on my discussions with them during a recent project.

As for individuals, it would be impossible to mention them all but I should like to single out Meg Sweet of The National Archives whose support over the last few years has seen me through some difficult times.

Kelvin Smith

Part 1

Preparation

1

Underlying principles

This chapter describes general principles of records and information management – those that are relevant to all records in whatever format. An understanding of such principles is essential to the implementation of electronic records management systems. It summarizes each of the seven principles and examines each one in turn.

- *Principle 1*   It is difficult to imagine – especially for those of us who have been in work for thirty years or more – how we managed before the use of computers became a fact of everyday life. Records managers, of course, were not the first professionals to realize the huge potential of the technology but within the past ten years or so electronic ways of working have become so embedded in the profession that we cannot manage without them. At the same time we must recognize that the technology is principally available as a tool to enable us to undertake our work more effectively and efficiently. We should not allow it to rule us. The technological skills of information and communications technology (ICT) staff will be necessary but a records management system must be overseen and managed by the records manager. The boundaries of records and information management and information technology management have become blurred in recent years. More and more records managers have ICT knowledge and skills, and more and more ICT practitioners have records management knowledge and skills. Each profession needs to work in partnership to the benefit of both.
- *Principle 2*   In the past five to ten years there have been two major driving forces in building effective records and information management systems and procedures: in the public sector there has been Freedom of Information legislation (in the UK and many other countries); and in all sectors the development of electronic ways of working. However, this ignores the fact that

there is one driver that has been around for much longer – the need for ever more efficient business practices. Records management is, and has always been, capable of making a major contribution to achieving this. At the same time, however, it has been largely neglected. To some extent this has been the fault of the profession itself; it has had a somewhat passive and pessimistic approach to its marketing. It has always been conscious that businesses (and I use that word in its very broadest sense – public and private sector bodies) have other priorities, namely their core functions. This is not to say that records managers have not been absolutely convinced of the efficacy of the practices and procedures that they have put forward. Now that business is increasingly generated electronically and public authorities have to be more accountable and transparent, records management is coming into its own. Records management must be recognized as a specific corporate function.

- *Principle 3*   Before we can embark on the design and implementation of an electronic records management system, we need to know what records the organization creates and holds. An information survey or records audit, as it is often referred to, is a vital component of the process towards implementation. We need to link information with business processes and consider re-engineering some of those processes as a result. Many organizations will have gone through this procedure, perhaps in the context of an inspection, a change in functions, or a straightforward reorganization in the light of new visions or legislative requirements (such as freedom of information). Perhaps a simple records survey is all that is required. This will often be a straightforward inventory of the records held, in what format they are held, and various details about their retention, value and use. The purpose of the survey is – to state the obvious – to know what records are held by the organization. With that basic information, improvements to existing record-keeping systems or the implementation of new systems can then be undertaken.

- *Principle 4*   Once records are created they must be managed in a standard file classification scheme that everyone in the organization understands and can use easily. A standard organization-wide scheme is important. Separate systems for different departments are grossly inefficient; they lead to the duplication of information, uncertainties over what information is current, and, above all, a neglect of corporate business practices. In the move towards electronic ways of working, no organization would contemplate separate software and separate systems for different departments.

- *Principle 5*   Too many records are kept for too long. We need only keep those records that we need to run our businesses (and a few that will be of historical value). These are two important truths – for electronic records as much as for paper records, if not even more so. One, keeping records that you do not need wastes space, time and energy. Two, a robust disposal policy is at the heart of good records management and time must always be set aside to destroy worthless information. It is not as cheap as you might think to maintain masses of electronic information.

- *Principle 6*   Those records that *are* worth keeping, whether in the medium or long term, must be managed and preserved so that they continue to maintain their status as reliable and authentic records. Preservation and sustainability are key issues which have yet to receive their fair share of attention from records managers. In many ways this is understandable. The profession has been concentrating on setting up new electronic systems and compiling effective file plans and appraisal methodologies. Given the transient nature of the medium, however, these issues cannot be put off.
- *Principle 7*   It is all very well having a well-preserved, well-structured and efficient records management system but it must be accessible to users when and where they need the information. Delivery and presentation systems must be simple and easy to use but at the same time must protect sensitive and confidential information. In an electronic environment this is difficult to achieve and this is an area where integrated working with ICT experts is absolutely vital to the records manager.

Roles and responsibilities

Automation of office tasks has prompted a re-skilling of the workforce and a greater need for record-keeping awareness. Records management tasks are no longer performed only by records clerks and records managers. Individuals in the workplace perform them themselves – creating records, naming and filing documents and maintaining intellectual control over the information they use (instead of this being the province of specialist records management units or registries).

In many countries in the past few years the profession has developed competency frameworks – formal matrices describing those skills and knowledge that are required to manage records and information. Some of these frameworks are extremely complicated in that they attempt to cover the wider information management and information technology areas. The focus of this current work, however, is the design and implementation of electronic records management systems and as such concentrates on those skills required for records management, with a little extra for the technical side of things (recognizing that it is more efficient to work in partnership with those that have the technical skills and experience to overcome the challenges posed by hardware operation or software systems).

The work of people responsible for the creation and management of records will cover a great variety of specific tasks falling within broad groups of records management operations. The main types of work undertaken are:

- design and implementation of appropriate records management systems and procedures
- creation and maintenance of records in all formats
- classification and filing of records

- safeguarding records
- preparation of indexes and other finding aids to facilitate retrieval of information and records
- identification and retrieval of information held within records
- management of subordinate staff
- development and implementation of agreed appraisal policies and procedures
- preparation and implementation of record disposal schedules
- archiving and preservation.

Competencies describe what people do in the workplace at various levels and specify the standards for each of those levels; they identify the characteristics, knowledge and skills possessed or required by individuals that enable them to undertake their duties and responsibilities effectively and thus to achieve professional quality standards in their work; and they cover all aspects of records management performance – particular skills and knowledge, attitudes, communication, application and development. Three types of competency are required for record-keeping work (and for most other types of work):

- *Core competencies* – these are competencies relating to an organization's strategic priorities and values. They will be applicable to all records management staff.
- *Functional competencies* – these describe the role-specific abilities required and usually relate to professional or technical skills.
- *Managerial competencies* – these competencies reflect the activity and performance required in supervisory and managerial positions.

There may be a mix of skills associated with particular posts. The framework shown in the Appendix at the end of this book identifies the particular competencies in these three areas and allows for the development of a profile of the skills required for specific posts. This profile can be translated into pay and grading terms with the help of human resource specialists. For example, the competencies can be described at four levels of knowledge and expertise:

- *Learner* – requires some support; just beginning to need to demonstrate the competency
- *Threshold* – able to perform most aspects of a competency without supervision
- *Excellent* – consistently demonstrates very good performance in most aspects of the competency; coaching others in the competency is an important part of this level
- *Expert* – demonstrates outstanding performance in a competency at a complex level; viewed as superior by others (within the organization and outside it); creates the environment in which others can succeed in the competency.

Each one of the competencies can then be described at these four levels. The descriptions for each level are examples of the skills or knowledge that should be reached before qualifying for the particular level. In the case of the core and managerial competencies these descriptions might be considered as relatively standard across all sectors. The functional competencies, however, may be dependent on the strategic objectives and organizational management of particular organizations.

Each role in records management work can be described in terms of a 'competency profile' which indicates:

- the competencies required in the job (selected from the framework)
- the level of a competency which must be demonstrated in that job.

The framework is a tool that organizations can use or adapt to draw up their own role profiles. It can also be used to identify training and development needs (by assessing staff against role profiles) and to define the competencies required when recruiting new staff. Competency frameworks and role profiles work best when they are tailored to a particular organization. In this respect the framework offered here should serve as an effective starting point.

Corporate working

The basic aim when implementing electronic records management must be to support a better corporate organization of electronic documents and records, and establish practices which the end user will find helpful in organizing their own work and their interaction with documents produced by others. A useful model for thinking about the best way to apply good practice (see Figure 1.1) contains the following elements:

- *corporate workspace* – contains formal corporate documents that are shared across all, or a significant part, of the organization
- *workgroup workspace* – contains operational documents in use by the work team and which are shared at least among that team
- *personal workspace* – contains documents that are at present only of interest to the individual.

Figure 1.1 Corporate organization

Invariably the best way to tackle electronic records management is to take a modular and/or incremental approach, to improve control and lower project risk. The key point is to recognize that the transition to full electronic records management is a wider programme that must start from the situation in which an organization currently finds itself. It is more than the simple implementation of a piece of software.

There are still many people who do not trust electronic records enough to operate with them in a corporate setting. It is not something that will disappear with the next age generation; it has to be taken on board now if we are to meet business targets and discharge legal obligations. There are two examples that might illustrate this point:

1 *Destruction of records* – some organizations still insist on having written (and signed) certification when records are destroyed. Why was this laid down in the first place? – to prove that destruction had taken place and had been undertaken by an authorized person. An electronic communication, perhaps in the form of an e-mail, will do just as well. Electronic audit systems can prove – probably more conclusively – that that e-mail was sent and sent by the person it says sent it.

2 *Use of e-mail* – there is a common misconception that e-mail messages are an ephemeral form of communication, but in reality they are increasingly becoming the primary business tool for both internal and external working, and increasingly recognized as an effective way to discharge corporate responsibilities. The types of e-mail that might need to be managed as a record include discussions, information distributed to groups of people, agreement to proceed, and other exchanges relating to corporate decision making. Indeed, e-mail messages can provide evidence about why a particular course of action was followed, which means that it is necessary not just to capture the e-mail relating to the final decision but also those discussions that might indicate why one decision was made as opposed to another. This is certainly important in a business context but may also be vital in answering freedom of information requests. As soon as an e-mail message needs to be forwarded for information purposes, it should be considered as a record. Furthermore, as soon as an e-mail message has been identified as a record of a business transaction, it is important that the message is retained with other records relating to that particular business activity – on a corporate electronic records management system.

Organizations should have corporate records management policies, covering all their records in all formats. Policy statements are best kept short. About two sides of an A4 sheet of paper – certainly no more than three sides – are best. Many people will not have time to read more than this so it is vital to get important points across quickly and clearly.

It is important to distinguish between policies and procedures. These are sometimes confused. Procedures implement policies. Typical characteristics of policy statements are:

- mandate for all RM functions
- commitment to create, keep and manage records
- role of records management
- relationship to overall strategy
- roles and responsibilities
- framework for supporting standards, etc.
- monitor compliance
- review at regular intervals.

A model statement is to be found at the end of this chapter.

Records survey

The purpose of a records survey is – to state the obvious – to know what records are held by the organization. Many organizations are well aware of the paper records that they hold – they are there, in the storeroom, archive or wherever, to be seen – but they may be less certain about what electronic records they hold. There are hundreds or even thousands of people in the organization. Where are they keeping the electronic information? Is it on shared drives, portable disk drives, CDs, stand-alone databases? With this basic information about who holds what and where, improvements to record-keeping systems can be considered. Many forms have been devised as a vehicle for collecting this information; some are more complicated than others. Keep it simple.

There is also no need to draw up sophisticated reports that draw on the information gathered. Simply keep the information and draw on it as other records and information management issues are addressed.

Summary of the steps to take

The first step in undertaking a records survey is to obtain senior management support. This should take the form of a directive from the Chief Executive, informing staff that the sample is taking place and that they are expected to co-operate. The passage of the sample will be eased significantly with such a directive.

There should be a communication strategy. People need to know not only that a sample is taking place but also why it is necessary. It needs to be put into context. Consider what the best ways are to do this:

- departmental meetings
- newsletters
- intranet

- one-to-one discussions.

The process needs to include a timetable of visits. Don't just turn up one morning, but at the same time don't give the people in the department being surveyed so much notice that they forget about it. Two weeks maximum is usual.

Collect as much background information as possible. This might include:

- previous audits/inspections
- procedure manuals
- reports
- statistics
- file lists
- disposal schedules
- maps, plans, etc.
- inventories.

Collecting information during the survey is a time-consuming and labour-intensive exercise. There is no easy or quick way. There are two main methods:

1 *Physical observation*: a physical survey requires a visit to business areas to look into each item of records storage equipment, ask questions and complete a standard survey form. It is usually sufficient to sample a series or collection of records rather than examine every individual record. The physical survey needs to be planned carefully and executed with a minimum of disruption. An initial investigation to establish the whereabouts, ownership, volume and condition of the records may be required to make the procedure more effective. When the plan and timetable have been drawn up, the detailed survey can take place. Four main actions form the key to finding out information from the survey:
   —*Find* every storage place (including tops of cabinets, disks, commercial storage, under desks)
   —*Look* at all the records and information in the location
   —*Ask* questions until understanding is complete
   —*Record* the information acquired for future analysis.
2 *Questionnaire*: the use of questionnaires relies on individuals to complete them accurately and on time. Much time can be wasted chasing up missing questionnaires, and following up unclear information on completed, or partially completed, questionnaires. Questions must be framed so that they elicit relevant and accurate information. For example, there should be a balance of closed and open questions; and only one question must be asked at any one time.
   The best method of obtaining the necessary information is probably a combination of these, i.e.:
   — send the questionnaire to key personnel in each business area (the person who knows most about the records – not always the head of department or unit)

— ask them to complete the questionnaire as far as possible and retain it

— make an appointment (for up to one hour) at which the issues raised by the questionnaire can be discussed and clarified. An opportunity to look at some records is also available.

Who should undertake the survey? This depends on the size and complexity of the exercise. It may be too much for one person. It may require technical input from ICT staff. It may be a good training/development opportunity for new or inexperienced staff. The objectives must be borne in mind throughout the process. It is easy for the surveyor/questioner to go off on, or be led on to, a tangent.

Survey reports should be clear and straightforward. Recommended structure:

- Executive summary (this is often the only part of a report which many people will read, so it needs to highlight major issues and recommendations in a clear and concise way)
- Introduction and background (why the survey was commissioned, respective roles of the client and surveyor in the process)
- Methodology
- Findings (general and specific to business areas; data should be in annexes, e.g. people seen, file list, breakdown of storage equipment, etc.)
- Recommendations (if relevant, it is useful to push for the inclusion of one or more recommendations in the next corporate plan of the organization)
- Summary of recommendations (number and keep short/concise, referring to paragraphs in the main body of the report).

Finally, it is important to take action – the report should not be sitting on a shelf or desk gathering dust.

File plans

File classification schemes are best based on function. Functions do not change (unlike organizational structures); they move around, come and go, but essentially they are stable. Figures 1.2 and 1.3 illustrate how a file classification scheme might be constructed both in paper and electronic schemes; the terms used are common in the profession at present.

The design and implementation of file plans is looked at more closely in Chapter 6.

Appraisal

Appraisal methodologies have been developed over the past 50 years or so to provide a formal procedure for analysing the background to records so that decisions on their medium- or long-term retention can be reached. However, the methodologies

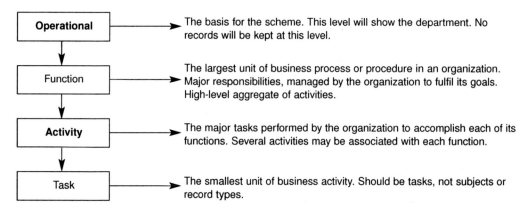

Operational → The basis for the scheme. This level will show the department. No records will be kept at this level.

Function → The largest unit of business process or procedure in an organization. Major responsibilities, managed by the organization to fulfil its goals. High-level aggregate of activities.

Activity → The major tasks performed by the organization to accomplish each of its functions. Several activities may be associated with each function.

Task → The smallest unit of business activity. Should be tasks, not subjects or record types.

Figure 1.2 File plan structure

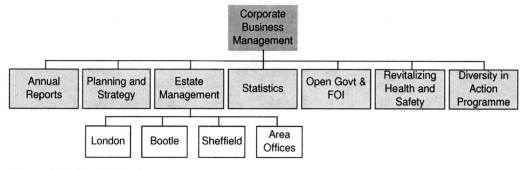

Figure 1.3 Sample file plan

used in paper records management will be difficult, if not impossible, to operate in an electronic environment, except in one key area – that of disposal scheduling. While we have been used to being able to review paper files individually to evaluate how long they should be kept, this is impractical with electronic records. For one thing, the number of records generated in electronic systems is far greater than in paper systems. For another, the medium is not conducive to the examination of documents one by one; sitting in front of a computer screen for long periods looking through the contents of folders is not good for anyone's health and safety.

We should bear in mind, however, that one principle of appraisal remains, whatever the medium. Deciding on what to keep and what to destroy is the same. It is the information that is being appraised, not the medium. There may be some easing of this singular approach (for example, in the electronic medium some records may be in a form that makes them inaccessible or even unusable, in which case there may be little point in selecting them for permanent preservation). The traditional adage of appraisal – that the principal reason for selecting records for permanent preservation is to preserve the history of the nation, community or organization – is losing ground to the inclusion of such criteria as use and cost in the process.

It is not just the historical perspective that is changing in this respect. The migration of electronic information to new formats can be an expensive and time-consuming process. More and more organizations are making pragmatic decisions and, after assessing business risks, are destroying information that cannot be read by the new systems which they have installed.

How long should records be kept? Records should be kept for as long as they are needed to meet the operational needs of the organization, together with legal and regulatory requirements. They need to be assessed to:

- determine their value as a source of information about the organization, its operations, relationships and environment
- assess their importance as evidence of business activities and decisions
- establish whether there are any legal or regulatory retention requirements.

Disposal schedules

Disposal schedules are the key element of the records appraisal process. The schedules cover series or collections of records for which a retention period can be determined for the whole series/collection. They identify and describe each record collection or series but not the individual records they contain. By taking into account the physical organization of records or the filing system in this way, disposal can be handled in blocks.

A disposal schedule should contain the following elements:

- the name of the department/operational area or unit
- a schedule reference number
- reference numbers (if applicable) of the records
- descriptions of the record series/collections
- disposal action/retention period
- date of the schedule
- signatures of the Records Manager and Business Manager. (If there is no formal records manager, the person with responsibility for managing records in the organization, and the person in the department/unit with responsibility for records).

The Records Manager should maintain a master set of all schedules and amendments/additions must be agreed with him/her before updated versions are issued.

Disposal schedules are crucial to good record keeping and are well worth the effort put in to produce them. Many public servants seem to have an in-built reluctance to destroy information ('. . . just in case'; 'it might come in useful . . .'). Be bold. Get rid of it, if it is of no further use. Of course, there will be a time when someone will ask for information which has been destroyed, but, if the truth be known, they can manage without it. You will have served the organization well and will have made a valuable contribution to effective corporate management.

Destruction

One of the great advantages of a corporate electronic records management system is that there is far less duplication than in a paper one. Most systems have version control as part of their operations and it is usually easy to be sure that you are dealing with the up-to-date version of a particular document. The general principle is that, where identified, duplicate records should be destroyed. Where information has been regularly shared between departments/units, only the original records should be retained in accordance with agreed guidelines. Care should be taken that seemingly duplicate records have not been annotated. Only one copy of each document should be kept as the corporate record.

We know in the UK public sector that under Freedom of Information legislation – more particularly the Code of Practice under section 46 of the Act – the destruction of information should be documented. This is good practice in any organization anywhere – principally to demonstrate accountability and transparency. By far the best way of doing this is to use disposal schedules. They are an effective instrument in showing that government or other information has been destroyed in accordance with proper practice and procedure.

Preservation

The term 'preservation' is used here as an overarching function aimed at securing the long-term survival of records. It encompasses physical and environmental storage, handling practices, reformatting of fragile series (by microfilm, digitization, etc.), conversion and migration (electronic records), and the physical repair of individual items (conservation). The function covers operations to ensure that records are stored, handled and managed so that their physical state, as well as the information they contain, is protected for as long as they are needed. This may be for posterity, or it may be for a fairly short retention period.

The preservation of information may be important for several reasons. It may be required in the medium and long term for managing current business processes. Long-term records, for example, may support strategic planning and decision making. They may be the corporate memory of the organization and may be instrumental in reducing duplication of work and in improving business efficiency. Information may also need to be kept for legal and related reasons – to provide transparency and accountability or to form part of a risk-management strategy. Then there is the historical aspect – records in all formats may have archival and historical research value.

Paradoxically, the concept of preservation must be at the forefront of the design of electronic records management systems. Electronic file formats encode information into a form that can only be processed and rendered comprehensible by very specific combinations of hardware and software. The accessibility of that information is therefore highly vulnerable in today's rapidly evolving technological environment. This issue is not solely the concern of archivists, but of all those responsible for managing and sustaining access to electronic records over even relatively short timescales. When designing an electronic records management system, therefore, the choice of file format should always be determined by the functional requirements of the record-creating process. However, record creators should be aware that long-term sustainability might be a requirement, both for ongoing business processes and archival preservation. Sustainability costs are inevitably minimized when these factors are taken into account prior to data creation – attempts to bring electronic records into a managed and sustainable regime after the fact tend to be expensive, complex and, generally, less successful.

Thus the practicality of managing any large collection of electronic records, whether in a business or archival context, is greatly simplified by minimizing the number of separate formats involved. It is highly desirable to identify the minimum set of formats that meet both the active business needs and sustainability requirements, and to restrict data creation to these formats.

Let us also not forget metadata in electronic systems. It seems obvious to state that metadata itself, which is critical for electronic records to retain their characteristics of content, context and structure, is also electronic. It is, therefore, subject to the same issues that affect other digital data – it is technology dependent and created on technology which is subject to upgrades and which may have been recreated on software which is no longer supported by its manufacturer. It requires careful management in order to ensure that it survives along with the records to which it is to lend reliability and authenticity.

The need to preserve electronic records generally becomes a real issue five years after their creation. The period of five years has come to be interpreted as 'long-term' in electronic terms and 'long term' is usually taken to be beyond one generation of technology. It certainly seems to be common experience that software systems are generally enhanced or have new versions within that time span. If electronic records are being kept for up to five years, it is usually safe enough to keep them in their original format. If records are being retained for longer than five years, it is advisable to use a standard format, either at creation or by conversion at the five-year stage. Standard formats generally recommended are:

- documents – PDF, plain text or XML
- spreadsheets – SQL
- databases – SQL
- pictures – TIFF.

The design of electronic records management systems must include a preservation strategy so that the records can be adequately managed over time and their continued accessibility can be assured. The development of such a strategy is examined in detail in Chapter 8.

Access

The main object of preserving information is so that it can remain accessible for future as well as present generations. In the electronic environment this link between preservation and access is more explicit in that both issues need to be addressed at the same time.

There are three key aspects to access in the design and implementation of electronic records management systems:

- *Accessibility* – information must be available to users and researchers when and where they need it
- *Usability* – systems must be simple and easy to use; users will not (to use current jargon) 'buy in' to a system if they have to make numerous changes to procedures and work patterns
- *Security* – systems must be able to protect sensitive and confidential information, and be trusted by users and stakeholders to do so.

Each of these aspects is examined more fully in Chapter 9.

In practical terms it would be rare for the access copy of a record to be the only copy of an electronic resource. Clearly the danger of the loss of vital information through damage or theft would be heightened were this to be the case. It is common practice in the UK for back-up copies to be made of current electronic resources but not so common for the same procedure to be taken with long-term electronic information, particularly that from five years after creation to preservation in a digital archive. Backing up electronic information can, however, be an expensive undertaking and organizations should consider a risk-assessment exercise. For example, they might ask themselves the following questions:

- is there a legal requirement to preserve the information?
- is the information rare or unique?
- is the information likely to be of historical value?
- in the event of loss or damage to the information, will it be impossible to obtain another copy from another source?
- is the information in a format that would not be described as 'standard'?

If the answers to these questions are 'yes', back-up copies should be made.

APPENDIX
Model records management policy statement
Scope

1   This policy provides for:
    — the requirements that must be met for the records of [*the organization*]
    to be considered as a proper record of the activity of the organization
    — the requirements for systems and processes that deal with records
    — the quality and reliability which must be maintained to provide a valuable
    information and knowledge resource for the organization
    — review of the policy and checking the quality of implementation
    — an overall statement of records management policy which is supplemented
    by detailed procedures.
    It covers records in all formats, created in the course of [*the organization's*] busi-
    ness, including non-conventional records.

Statement

2   Information is a corporate asset and the records of [*the organization*] are
    important sources of administrative, fiscal, legal, evidential and historical
    information. They are vital to the organization in its current and future
    operations, for the purposes of accountability, and for an awareness and
    understanding of its history. They are the corporate memory of the organization.
3   In consultation with organizations which may be concerned with the
    management of its records, [*the organization*] will create, use, manage and
    destroy or preserve its records in accordance with all statutory requirements.
4   Systematic records management is fundamental to organizational efficiency.
    It ensures that the right information is:
    — captured, stored, retrieved and destroyed or preserved according to need
    — fully exploited to meet current and future needs, and to support change
    — accessible to those who need to make use of it.
    and that the appropriate technical, organizational and human resource elements
    exist to make this possible.
5   All staff of [*the organization*] who create, use, manage or dispose of records
    have a duty to protect them and to ensure that any information that they add
    to the record is accurate, complete and necessary. All staff involved in managing
    records will receive the necessary training.
6   The records management policy is a specific part of [*the organization's*] overall
    corporate programme and relates to other policies, such as:
    — following best practice in specific areas
    — the organization's ICT strategy
    — data protection.

Accountability

7 The *Chief Executive* has a duty to ensure that [*the organization*] complies with the requirements of legislation affecting management of the records, and with supporting regulations and codes.

8 The *Records Manager* will work closely with Heads of Departments to ensure that there is consistency in the management of records and that advice and guidance on good records management practice is provided.

9 *Managerial and technical staff* are responsible for ensuring that records and information systems in their areas conform to this policy and to the requirements of legislation. *All members of staff* are responsible for documenting their actions and decisions in the records and for maintaining the records in accordance with good records management practice.

Monitoring compliance

10 [*the organization*] will follow this policy within all relevant procedures and guidance used for operational activities. Interpretation of the policy will be monitored and there will be regular planned inspections by Quality Services staff and Internal Auditors to assess how the policy is being put into practice. These inspections will seek to:

— identify areas of good practice which can be used throughout [*the organization*]

— highlight where non-conformance to the procedures is occurring

— if appropriate, recommend a tightening of controls and make recommendations as to how compliance can be achieved.

2

Context

This chapter examines how useful and relevant it is to describe the context in which records management functions are undertaken in the organization, the legal framework in which it operates and factors (internal and external) affecting records management – all as a precursor to developing the business case for electronic records management and planning the system itself.

Definitions

We first of all need to define what we mean by various terms so that there is a clear description of the context of electronic records management and an analysis of the functional arrangements in an organization that can be easily understood. The simplest way to do that is to set out a glossary of terms. The glossary that follows tries to be comprehensive and to indicate preferred terms but it is recognized that you may well come across some terms not covered here. Working cultures in organizations – sometimes but not always split on sectoral lines – adopt different terms for a variety of undertakings. The aim here is not to deliver an analysis of such cultural differences but to steer you towards acceptable handles that will allow you to get on and do the job.

Glossary of terms

Accession

Completion of a set of intellectual and physical processes required to effect the transfer of custody and/or ownership of records from the creating or other responsible agency to the archive repository or agency for permanent retention and perpetual access.

Aggregation

Assembly of records or documents at various levels of the file plan. In the paper environment the most familiar assembly is the file; in local area networks it is typically a folder or sub-folder; in e-mail systems it is likely to be an inbox.

Appraisal

The process of distinguishing records of continuing value from those of no further value so that the latter may be eliminated.

Archival repository

A building or part of a building in which archives are preserved and made available for consultation.

Archives

Records of enduring value selected for permanent preservation.

Authenticity

An authentic record is one that can prove to be what it purports to be, to have been created or sent by the person purported to have created or sent it, and to have been created or sent at the time purported.

Class

A subdivision of a classification scheme by which the file plan is organized. It will usually comprise a folder but that folder may not necessarily contain records – it may simply be used to construct the file plan into an acceptable hierarchy.

Classification scheme

A scheme which categorizes records into assemblies (*see* Aggregation) that are designed to preserve the business context. Often referred to as a business classification scheme.

Current records

Records regularly used for the conduct of the current business of an organization or individual.

Declaration

The process of defining that a document and its metadata comprise a corporate record.

Deliverable unit

A constituent part of a record that is logically deliverable and possesses a unique reference, e.g. web page, folder, e-mail, document, disk, tape, file or film.

Digital archive

The depository of original accessioned electronic records. Also known as a digital object store.

Digital object

The electronic record in its original format that is accessioned into the archival repository.

Disposal schedule

A document describing the recurring records of an organization, specifying which records should be preserved permanently as having enduring value, and authorizing on a continuing basis and after the lapse of specified retention periods or the occurrence of specified actions or events, the disposal by destruction or other means of the remaining records.

Document

Recorded information stored on a physical medium (paper, microfilm, electronic, etc.) that can be interpreted. In an electronic context, it is that WORD document in a folder, a spreadsheet, an e-mail in an inbox and so on. Several documents make up a record, although it may be possible (if there is sufficient context) for one document to be a record.

Electronic document

A document created, housed or transmitted by electronic rather than physical means, and which satisfies the definition of a document.

Electronic record

A record created, housed or transmitted by electronic rather than physical means, and which satisfies the definition of a record. A record can consist of one or more objects, e.g. web page, file, folder, e-mail or document.

Electronic records management system (ERM)

A system that manages electronic records throughout their life cycle, from creation and capture through to their destruction or permanent retention, and that retains their integrity and authenticity while ensuring that they remain accessible. The term is used here to include similar systems such as electronic document management (EDM) systems, electronic document and records management (EDRM) systems and enterprise content management (ECM) systems, although it is recognized that there are subtle differences (see page 57).

Emulation

Software used to mimic hardware or software that preserves the original appearance of and preserves access to electronic records.

Export

The process of passing copies of a record or group of records with their metadata from one system to another. Unlike transfer, it does not necessarily mean the removal of the records from the first system.

File

As far as possible this term has been avoided in the following pages because of the confusion it causes. In the paper world it refers to an assembly or aggregation of documents or records; in the electronic environment it is often used (in records management) to describe a folder or even an application in the computer system.

File plan

The structure resulting from a systematic identification and arrangement of business activities and the records they generate into categories according to logical conventions, methods and procedural rules. It is, in effect, a representation of the business of an organization which is best suited to support the conduct of that business and accord with records management principles.

Folder

This is the primary unit of management for electronic records – a container for the electronic documents. It is also used in e-mail systems. There may also be sub-folders in the file plan or other scheme.

Hybrid record

A record that comprises paper and electronic documents (and stored accordingly) which must be managed together.

Information registry

A repository for metadata related to digital records but not specific records.

Integrity

The integrity of a record refers to its being complete and unaltered. An authorized annotation, addition or deletion of a record should be explicitly indicated and traceable.

Interoperability

Coherent exchange of information and services between systems.

Manifestation

A copy or version of a record which has been created for a number of reasons, e.g. original accession, redaction, migrated version, version for presentation purposes, hidden sensitive information. A record may therefore have multiple manifestations.

Metadata

Contextual information about a record. Data describing context, content and structure of records and their management through time. Metadata is structured information that enables us to describe, locate, control and manage other information.

Migration

Transfer of electronic records from one system to another while maintaining the records' authenticity, integrity, reliability and usability; the content (although not always the original look and feel) is preserved.

National Archives

The archival repository in which archives of the central institutions of the [country] are preserved and made available for consultation.

Open-source software

Software where the code used to create digital objects is in the public domain.

Presentation

The process of publishing records from an electronic records management system – for presentation outside that environment but by methods within its control (for example, on a website).

Preservation

Processes and operations involved in ensuring technical and intellectual survival of authentic records through time. The preservation of electronic records is usually referred to as digital preservation.

Protective marking

Designations applied to a record showing the level of security that it should be afforded (for example, Restricted, Confidential, Secret).

Record

Recorded information regardless of form or medium created, received and maintained by any organization or individual in the pursuance of its legal obligations or in the transaction of its business and providing evidence of the performance of those obligations or that business.

Records centre

A building designated for the low-cost storage, maintenance and communication of semi-current records pending their eventual disposal.

Redaction

The process of removing, withholding or hiding parts of a record due either to the application of freedom of information exemptions or to a decision by an archive to restrict access where sensitivity, copyright or data protection issues arise.

Reliability

A reliable record is one whose contents can be trusted as a full and accurate representation of the transaction, activities or facts to which they attest and can be depended upon in the course of subsequent transactions or activities.

Rendition

Translation of a record into another software format by a process within the control of an electronic records management system, without loss of content.

Resource discovery

Information retrieval – usually in the electronic environment.

Retention schedule

See Disposal schedule

Review

The examination of the disposal status of a record to determine whether its disposal can now be determined

Semi-current records

Records required only infrequently for the conduct of current business; for the purposes of the legislation files and other assemblies of records on which no action has been recorded for five years are usually regarded as semi-current records.

Sustainability

Preservation for business purposes as opposed to archival preservation.

Technology watch

Programme that monitors changes in the technical environment likely to affect the management of electronic records.

Transfer

The process of exporting electronic records and subsequently destroying them within the exporting system, thereby transferring custody of the records.

Usability

A usable record is one that can be located, retrieved, presented and interpreted.

XML

EXtensible mark-up language – used for the definition of data formats and important in the transfer of metadata.

Strategic context

In order to ensure corporate support, electronic records management must relate to the strategic context of the organization – its IT strategy, business strategy and policy objectives set by government and similar institutions. While a strategy plan may not in itself be a recipe for success, no organization can operate successfully without one. Managers and their staff are often so preoccupied with day-to-day issues and operations that they lose sight of the organization's corporate objectives. A good strategic plan should provide the basis for more detailed planning (like the introduction of electronic records management systems), serve as a framework for giving support to business operations and assist in the monitoring of performance.

Strategic planning often comprises clearly defined steps:

Vision

The vision needs to be a picture of the organization in three to five years' time, taking into account its processes, products, customers, staffing, etc. How large will it be? What will its activities be? What will it look like? In simple terms the vision arises from the identification of the distance between 'where we are' and 'where we want to be'. We need to be sure where we are in business terms and then choose where we want to be – the vision. A clear vision of what the future holds for the organization will help to make the implementation of an electronic records management programme a success.

Mission

The nature of the organization can be expressed in terms of its mission. This should indicate its purposes – a statement that shows what the organization's business is about. For example:

> . . . to design, develop, manufacture and market electronic records management systems that meet accepted international standards and meet the needs of customers in both private and public sectors. The systems integrate the company's proprietary software with

hardware supplied by major manufacturers, and are sold to all types of organizations in the private and public sectors. The systems are distinguished by operations that permit use without trained data-processors.

Values

Values are 'softer' than mission statements. They cover the operation of the business of the organization and its conduct or relationships with customers, suppliers, employees or a particular community. They concern not the 'What' of what an organization does – the strategy and mission – but the 'How'. It is a statement of what an organization stands for and believes in; what its employees expect of each other and aim to provide for customers, whoever they may be. For example, the following is an extract from a statement by The National Archives (2006):

- *Putting customers first*
  — Provide a great service to *all* our customers
  — Ask, listen, do
  — Deliver what customers need
  — Make complex things simple
  — Our success is satisfied customers
- *Working together*
  — One team with shared goals
  — Discuss, agree and support
  — Everyone's important: we all know what to do and how we contribute to success
  — Respect and trust given and earned
  — A duty of care and courtesy to each other
  — Diverse backgrounds and views make a stronger organization
  — We learn from others' success and celebrate our own.

Objectives

These are the results that the organization wants to achieve in the period covered by the planning process. They are generally set out in two timeframes – the business year and the strategic planning period (up to five years). Objectives relate to the expectations and requirements of stakeholders, including employees and customers, and reflect the underlying reasons for running the organization. For example, the following is an extract from The National Archives Strategic Plan (2007–8):

We will produce a range of case studies showing the economic, social, academic, policy and public service benefits of re-using public sector information by April 2008.

Establish appropriate processes to ensure the survival of digital surrogate records that have continued business value.

Programmes

The final element of strategic planning is usually the programmes, which set out the organization's implementation plans for the key strategies (such as electronic records management). These will cover resources, deadlines, budgets and performance targets.

Organizational context

There are two essential elements to the function of records management:

* it covers records in all formats (paper, electronic, oral, film, microform, etc.)
* it covers records from the moment that they are created until their disposal (either by destruction or preservation in an archive).

Records management is a corporate function in a similar way to human resources, finance and estates management. It should be recognized as a specific corporate programme within an organization and it should receive the necessary levels of organizational support to ensure effectiveness. It needs to bring together responsibilities for records in all formats from their creation to their ultimate disposal. While you might expect that moves towards electronic records management would make this almost a natural progression, in practice electronic ways of working have had the opposite effect. Records have become more dissipated than ever in some areas. E-mail systems have evolved separately from document and other management systems. Stand-alone databases are still being created and managed separately from shared drives and document management systems. The result is, at best, disjointed ways of working and an inability to locate information as and when required, and, at worst, chaos. It will not be possible to plan and implement electronic records management systems without the basic records management infrastructure in place. There must be an understanding and an awareness of good record keeping and the effective management of records and information in current (usually paper) systems before embarking on the electronic path. Get the paper systems working effectively and efficiently, *then* think about electronic working.

All organizations produce records but many do not have a designated records manager with prime responsibility for ensuring an effective and efficient approach to managing records and information across the organization. The person or persons responsible for the records management function in your organization should also have responsibility for, or close organizational connection with, the person or persons responsible for other information management issues, such as freedom of information, and privacy/data protection. This organizational connection should also be extended towards information and communication technology (ICT) units. In the design of information management systems – from simple databases to electronic records management file plans – both the records management and ICT professionals have important roles to play. Such co-operation will ensure progress towards the implementation of effective records and information management systems that accord with legislation and business practices, and will ensure that the best use is made of the latest technology. The person with responsibility for records management should be someone of appropriate seniority, someone who knows the organization well and can promote and implement the functional requirements. Everyone in your organization should know who the records manager is. The role needs to be formally acknowledged and made known throughout the organization – from top to bottom.

The precise location of the records management function in an organization's hierarchy is largely a matter for local determination. The important thing is that it is recognized as a corporate function.

Business analysis

The overall purpose of creating, using and managing records is to support the business of the organization. These business needs – the benefits which the organization expects to gain, for example, from a move to electronic working – and other relevant external requirements on the organization are the general determinants of the way in which records should be organized, and the means by which they may be accessed. The word 'business' in this context is used in its more general sense of any purposeful work or activity rather than in its more particular sense as commercial trade.

While it is not the central theme of this book, it may be useful to make some comments about business analysis. The process involves identifying and then examining the component parts of an organization, in order to gain information about how the organization functions and the relationships between various tasks, jobs, people, structures and other elements. This includes identifying broad organizational goals and supporting business areas and processes, and business process definition and decomposition. You will often find that these analytical projects can lead to enhanced performance in your organization by improving the way work is carried out. For example, available resources can be linked more directly to the aims and goals of the organization; and similarly records and information systems can function more effectively if they are more closely linked with the institution's day-to-day work.

Business analysis allows managers to see their organizations as an integrated whole, preventing them from getting lost in the complexity of the organizational structure or the details of their day-to-day job. When managers apply such thinking to an understanding of their organization, they see that the best performance will be achieved when all the component parts of the organization, or business system, are working together harmoniously to achieve the organization's mission and objectives. Optimum performance can only be achieved when organizational change or redesign takes into account the entire system – the corporate whole. Many projects aimed at redesigning record-keeping systems fail because they are not integrated with and do not support other organizational systems.

Two good examples of the business analysis process are:

1 *DIRKS (Design and Implementation of Record Keeping Systems)*
   The DIRKS methodology, developed some years ago by The National Archives
   of Australia, is an eight-step process for the improvement of record-keeping and
   information management practices. Practical guidance on using the methodology
   is in the DIRKS Manual, which includes a step (B) on the analysis of a business
   activity. See the website of The National Archives of Australia (www.naa.gov.au/
   recordkeeping/dirks/summary.html).
2 *JISC (Joint Information Systems Committee)*
   JISC commissioned a study of the records life cycle in 1999. An integral part
   of this study was the business function activity model (FAM). It was drawn up
   originally as part of an overall functional approach to records management for
   higher education authorities. It presents a very practical approach to business
   analysis, and was recently revised. See the JISC website (www.jisc.ac.uk).

Even if there is no comprehenive reorganization of business functions underway,
records managers can still use business analysis as a tool to restructure record-
keeping operations and develop file plans and disposal schedules, as well as
carrying out a number of other projects designed to improve records management.
To succeed at redesigning record-keeping systems, records managers must become
adept at working with people in all parts of the organization. Just as senior
management must remember to include records professionals in organization-wide
business analysis activities, records managers and archivists must also include other
stakeholders – including programme managers, information technology specialists,
information managers, legal experts, internal auditors and others – in the analysis
of records systems.

Compliance context

All organizations need to be aware of, and to be able to identify, the legal and
regulatory environments in which they operate, which affect the requirement to
document their activities (and thus the management of their records and
information). Many organizations have a legal requirement to provide certain
information as well as adequate evidence of compliance with particular laws and
regulations. The records management policy of an organization should reflect the
application of relevant laws and regulations to its business processes.

In the context of the management of information the regulatory environment
in the UK consists of:

• statute and case laws (for example, Companies Act 1985; Public Records Act
  1958; Freedom of Information Act 2000; Data Protection Act 1998)

- regulations, usually covering specific sectors and business environments (for example, Control of Substances Hazardous to Health Regulations 2002; Construction (Design and Management) Regulations 1994; local financial regulations)
- standards (for example, the international standard on Records Management, ISO 15489; quality management and quality assurance standards, B ISO 9000)
- codes of practice (for example, Code of Practice on the Management of Records under Freedom of Information 2002).

We might also include in this list the expectations of society of what is acceptable behaviour for the specific sector or organization.

Where specific types of organization are required by law to create and keep records of particular activities there may sometimes be issues concerning the medium of the record that have to be taken into account. These are often connected with legal admissibility – for example, should the record be hard copy only, a hard copy that is scanned into an electronic records management system (then used electronically) or a record that is electronic throughout its life cycle?

Disposal

Three areas are heavily regulated – finance, health and safety, and human resources – and compliance usually means careful management and disposal of records, in whatever format. In the matter of disposal, cognizance needs to be taken of the Limitation Act 1980. This legislation lays down periods after which legal action cannot be taken in respect of different kinds of transactions, for example:

- financial: 6 years
- land: 12 years.

For records managers this means that some records created by these functional areas might need to be kept for the stated periods to meet any claims for damages, etc. Essentially this is a risk-assessment process (what are the risks of receiving claims where records have been destroyed?) and a cost-analysis process (do the costs of preserving records outweigh the cost of any claim that might have to be met?).

Also in the matter of disposal, there is the situation when an organization is involved in litigation or similar processes such as dispute resolution. An organization will need to rely on records as evidence to support its case. If records have been disposed of, or incomplete records have been kept, the ability to bring a claim, or defend one, may be severely compromised.

Access

Attitudes to the access of information – particularly in the public sector – have changed dramatically in recent years. Increasingly, members of the public have come to expect to be told or have the right to find out how their money is being spent, what is being done in their name, or how their investment is being managed. Paradoxically, they are also concerned that personal data about individuals are adequately protected.

Freedom of Information Act 2000

The Freedom of Information Act 2000 is intended to promote a culture of openness and accountability among public authorities by providing people with rights of access to the information held by them. It is expected that these rights will facilitate better public understanding of how public authorities carry out their duties, why they make the decisions they do and how they spend public money. The Act covers the whole of the public sector and those parts of the private sector that discharge public functions. It imposes significant duties and responsibilities on these organizations. These include:

- knowing what information they hold
- managing their information holdings effectively
- having in place the infrastructure for dealing with FOI requests
- meeting challenging deadlines in responding to individual requests for information
- proactively disseminating information through a publication scheme
- setting up arrangements to handle complaints and appeals
- ensuring consistency in discharging their duties under the Act.

Freedom of information legislation is only as good as the quality of the records that are subject to its provisions. Statutory rights of access such as this are of little use if reliable records and information are not created in the first place, if they cannot be found when needed, or if the arrangements for their eventual archiving or destruction are inadequate. It is likely that the implementation of electronic records management will increase the pressure on the record-keeping system.

Data Protection Act 1998

Data protection legislation has been in existence since 1984. An Act of that year required all organizations processing data about individuals electronically to register the existence of their databases with the Data Protection Registrar. The 1998 Act extends the definition of personal data to include paper records and sets out eight principles with which data controllers (the people responsible for determining the purpose for which personal data are processed) have to comply:

- Processing of data must be fair and lawful
- Data must be obtained for a specified and lawful purpose, and not be further

processed in any manner incompatible with that purpose
- Data must not be excessive
- Data must be accurate and kept up to date
- Data must not be kept longer than necessary
- The data subject must be told when and what data are being processed, the purposes for which data are being processed, the recipients to whom the data may be disclosed, and (in some cases) the source of the data
- Data must be protected against unauthorized or unlawful processing or loss, destruction or damage
- Data must not be transferred outside the European Union unless to a country or area where the rights of data subjects can be adequately protected.

Human Rights Act 1998

The main provisions of the Human Rights Act came into force on 2 October 2000. The implications for records and information management centre on Articles 8 and 10 of the Act:

- *Article 8: Right to respect for private and family life*
  Everyone has the right to respect for his private and family life, his home and correspondence. There shall be no interference by a public authority with the exercise of this right except such as in accordance with the law and is necessary in a democratic society in the interests of national security, public safety or the economic well-being of the country, for the prevention of disorder or crime, for the protection of health or morals, or for the protection of the rights and freedoms of others.
- *Article 10: Freedom of expression*
  Everyone has the right to freedom of expression. This right shall include freedom to hold opinions and to receive and impart information and ideas without interference by public authority and regardless of frontiers. . . . The exercise of these freedoms, since it carries with it duties and responsibilities, may be subject to such formalities, conditions, restrictions or penalties as are prescribed by law and are necessary in a democratic society, in the interests of national security, territorial integrity or public safety, for the prevention of disorder or crime, for the protection of health or morals, for the protection of the reputation or rights of others, for preventing the disclosure of information received in confidence, or for maintaining the authority and impartiality of the judiciary.

Standards and Codes of Practice

There are many standards, codes of practice and other guidelines that are concerned with records and information management. Although most do not have legal status, they are nonetheless powerful tools which allow us to demonstrate the qualities of transparency and authenticity which are increasingly required in the record-keeping profession.

ISO 15489

The international standard on records management promotes the standardization of policies and procedures to ensure that 'appropriate attention and protection is given to all records, and that the evidence and information they contain can be retrieved more efficiently and effectively'. It provides guidance on the whole range of record management activities – the creation, capture and management of records – in all formats. Specifically within a regulatory context it makes the point that proper management of records enables any organization to:

- meet legislative and regulatory requirements including archival, audit and oversight activities
- provide protection and support in litigation including the management of risks associated with the existence of, or lack of, evidence of organizational activity
- protect the interests of the organization and the rights of employees, clients and present and future stakeholders.

Accompanying the Standard is a Technical Report that explains how the desired standards might be implemented in practice.

Code of Practice on the Management of Records under FOI

The Code of Practice under section 46 of the Freedom of Information Act 2000 lays down best practice for the management of information, in all formats, by public authorities from the moment it is created to the time of its disposal (whether this is by destruction or preservation in an archive). Although the Code has been published in the context of freedom of information, its contents describe efficient business practice for the management of records by public authorities in whatever area they may be operating.

The Code is an important and highly significant document in the development of the records management profession. It provides an effective framework within which policies and procedures can be drawn up and much of what it says can be incorporated into private-sector policies and procedures.

Legal admissibility

Since many important records are now created and held electronically, it is important that, should these be required as evidence in a court of law, their authenticity can be proved. Electronic records are particularly vulnerable to tampering because it is possible to make additions or deletions that are not apparent to the viewer of the document. It can also be difficult to tell the difference between the original, authentic record and copies of it, which may have been altered. The British Standards Institute has published BIP 0008, *Code of Practice on the Legal Admissibility and Evidential Weight of Information Stored Electronically*, which provides comprehensive guidance on this issue.

Others

In the UK health sector the Department of Health has recently published *Records Management: NHS Code of Practice*. This succeeds and replaces previous guidance contained in the Department of Health circular HSC 053/1999 *For the Record*. The Code provides a key component of information governance arrangements for the National Health Service in the UK.

PD 0010 Principles of Good Practice for Information Management identifies features common to all information-handling processes, independent of specific technological devices, setting out five principles which would remain applicable however much the technology changes. The principles are to:

- recognize and understand all types of information
- understand the legal issues and exercise 'duty of care' responsibilities
- identify and specify business processes and procedures
- identify enabling technologies to support business processes and procedures
- monitor and audit business processes and procedures.

ISO 17799 Code of practice for information security management – has been explicitly produced for an environment which is increasingly confronted by a range of threats (fraud, espionage, sabotage, vandalism – the list is almost endless). Much of the detail of the standard is for ICT professionals but even this has to be backed up by appropriate procedures in records and information management.

Copyright

Records and information management should also address the issue of copyright. More often than not there is specific copyright legislation and the organization should take into account the impact in respect of copyright in records and information that it holds. For example, if it provides access to its records (such as in an archival institution) and provide copies of them, it must do so without breach of any private copyrights that may subsist in them.

3

Making a business case for ERM

This chapter examines the procedures required to make a business case for electronic records management. It makes a couple of assumptions – that the underlying principles described in Chapter 1 are more or less in place in the organization and that the context or functional analysis described in Chapter 2 has been completed (the report of which will form an annex to or part of the business case itself).

Introduction

Top managers and financial directors in all organizations need to be convinced that it is worth committing resources or spending large sums of money on projects such as electronic records management before they will give them their blessings. The business case, therefore, is a crucial document. Before committing anything to paper (or screen!), you need to be clear about the purpose and objective of the business case. The purpose is to set out all the implications for the organization in going ahead with such a project, while the objective is to gain organizational commitment to this. It should not be limited to gaining permission to take a longer look at the suggestion to introduce electronic records management; it needs to be stronger than that.

All business cases should cover the following points:

- what is the current situation on records and information management?
- why should the organization go ahead with the project?
- what will happen if the organization does not go ahead with the project?
- what are the alternatives (if any)?
- what is happening in records and information management in similar organizations in the same sector?
- what are the benefits accruing from the project?

- what is the cost of the project?
- what demands on other organizational resources will there be?

While business cases are very individual documents and will vary greatly according to the organizational context, much can be learnt from the experiences of other organizations that have gone through the process of planning and implementing electronic records management systems. It is worthwhile investigating to see if any case studies are available and whether any work undertaken by others might be re-used or modified for your own purposes.

Who will undertake the compilation of the business case? Consider whether it might be undertaken by one person or a project team (the size of the organization will usually be a determining factor). Whoever it is, particular skills and knowledge will be required. For example, in a team set-up there will need to be expertise in records management principles and procedures; if interviewing staff is a key element, there will need to be someone particularly adept at eliciting information and possessing good interpersonal skills; almost certainly there will need to be an information technology expert or at least access to such expertise.

What resources are required to undertake the business case? These may be one or more of the following:

- time
- project methodology
- corporate plans and other documents
- access to file servers
- information on electronic records management systems (requirements, previous studies, undertakings in similar organizations, etc.).

Step by step

Business cases are easier to compile and, most important, easier to understand if they are structured in such a way as to reflect the incremental nature of a large project such as the implementation of electronic records management. A step-by-step approach is therefore recommended as follows:

1 Introduction

The introduction should refer to supporting sections of the Corporate Business Plan and state its origins (for example, that it is the result of an investigation into the organization's records management systems arising from the need to comply with particular requirements, such as the Code of Practice on the Management of Records under section 46 of the Freedom of Information Act 2000, or the international standard on records management, ISO 15489). It should also set out the structure of the business case and confirm the model by which it has been guided (internal or external).

2   Current situation

A vital consideration for the second step is whether the readers of the business case are likely or not to be familiar with the current situation on records and information management. Do you have the kind of organization in which senior management is aware of procedures, difficulties and achievements at the operational end of the business? Or do you have a management team that is remote from such matters? This is an important judgement to make at this stage. You will want to engage the readers from the start. Let's be frank – this is not going to be the most exciting document that will cross the desks or computers of senior management during the year; but we know how crucial it might be for the future of the organization and we have to persuade the readers that this is so.

If you have a fully involved management, you will not want to tell them anything that they are already aware of. They will be more interested in the 'why and how' rather than the 'what'. They are looking for evidence in support of the statements that you make rather than accepting them at face value. With this in mind the following questions ought to be addressed in an assessment of the current situation:

- the role of records management in the corporate set-up – is it recognized as a specific corporate programme or is it somewhat detached from a recognizable role within the organization?
- what organizational connections (if any) with similar functions, such as data protection, freedom of information and information technology, does records management have in the organization?
- how is the organization's records management policy (if any) implemented?
- against what standards is records management performance measured?
- is there a qualified records manager or someone with formal responsibility for the management of the organization's records?
- are records in all formats (paper, film, electronic) covered by the role?
- does the role include responsibility for records throughout their life cycle?
- does the person responsible for records management have ready access to the senior management team?
- what is the current system for capturing information in the organization (paper filing, classification scheme, local area network, databases, e-mail, etc.)?
- how are records stored and maintained?
- what measures are in place to protect sensitive information?
- what are the procedures for the appraisal and disposal of information?
- what plans (if any) are in place to ensure the long-term use of electronic information?

- are regular reports on records management in the organization made and submitted to management?
- to what extent are records covered in the organization's disaster recovery or business continuity plan?
- what records management training initiatives and awareness programmes are in place?

The assessment might include a report on any functional analysis that you may have undertaken (see Chapter 2). It is usually preferable to include such a report as an annex to the business case and refer to it in the narrative.

It may also be useful to include in the assessment other relevant documents or links to such documents, like the records management policy statement (if any), the disaster recovery plan, records management standards (for example ISO 15489, the international standard on records management), internal audit or other reports and risk assessments. If your organization has none of these documents (or only one or two), this is an opportunity to point out that fact and to cite those standards and best practices that recommend them (for example, ISO 15489 or, in the UK, the FOI Act section 46 Code of Practice on Records Management).

In making this assessment a good and practical way of gathering the required information is to draw up a set of key questions for each of the areas that you need to investigate. These should be supported by supplementary questions that are designed to gather the evidence in which senior management will be most interested. For example:

Key question
Does the organization have a records management policy?

Supplementary questions
Is the policy separate or part of a wider information policy?
How long is the policy?
How is the policy distributed or made known to the staff of the organization?
How often is the policy reviewed/updated?
Does it cover records in all formats?
How is the policy implemented?
How is implementation measured?
Etc.

3 Overview of ERM Systems

Readers of the business case may or may not have an appreciation of electronic records management systems. The detail into which you might wish to go in this third step will depend on the existence of or how deep is this appreciation.

Five main areas should be covered:

- *The current state of the profession* – in the past 30 years or so an increasing amount of business and government activity has been conducted electronically. Communication of information has increasingly been undertaken through e-mail and the internet. The most significant way in which these changes have affected records management is the danger they can pose to the continued security and accessibility of the electronic information. Important data can be lost through the lack of an adequate management system for electronic records, obsolescent hardware and the introduction of new, or new versions of, software. The underlying principles of records management hold good in this area for electronic records in just the same way as they do for paper records. Records (in whatever format) are an indispensable element of the accountability that public-sector bodies have to show to government and similar institutions or that private-sector organizations need to show to shareholders and others. Records show whether organizations or individuals have met defined legal or business obligations. They are an indispensable tool in the decision-making process of all organizations. Thus electronic records – all records – need to:
  — enable an organization to retain a corporate memory of its various activities
  — provide an auditable trail of transactions
  — demonstrate accountability for actions
  — fulfil legal obligations.
  Apart from technical obsolescence, many electronic record types cannot be fully represented on paper – for example, a spreadsheet must be printed twice to preserve both data and formulae; a hypertext document with many links can only be partially printed – so there is no alternative to managing (and perhaps preserving) the information electronically.
- *Current developments elsewhere in the sector* – what is happening in your particular part of the public or private sector? For example, in the UK central government a White Paper (policy document) called *Modernising Government* was published in 1999. The section of this headed 'Information Age Government' included the directive that '. . . by the year 2004 all newly-created public records will be electronically stored and retrieved'. Since 1999 very many government departments have accordingly introduced electronic records management systems. Very often what has been undertaken in some parts of your sector inevitably means that it needs to be followed by all participants.
- *Rationale of electronic records management* – a likely question from the readers of the business case is 'why should the organization move towards electronic ways of managing its information?' If the first area of this step does not convince them, you may want to give some detail about the purpose and efficacy of electronic records management systems. This falls under two headings – tactical benefits and strategic benefits. The whole area of the benefits that can accrue from the introduction of an electronic records management system is examined separately below (see Benefits).
- *Cost* – some overview of the cost of electronic records management systems might

be given, if they are unlikely to be known. This should include capital and ongoing (for example, licensing and maintenance) costs. Detailed costs of the specific project that you will be recommending to your organization will be dealt with separately (see Costs).

- *Market capability* – Standard practice in most projects is to collect data that will enable a decision to be made on whether to offer a project to the market. This necessitates an examination of the capability to deliver and the motivation to deliver. These involve:
  — whether suppliers can deliver within any constraints you might set
  — whether the end product would be sufficiently reliable
  — whether the end product would represent value for money
  — whether the market will support the proposal.
  The simplest way of collecting this data is through the internet and by contacting suppliers of electronic records management systems. You may want, for example, to examine and test systems, attend exhibitions and demonstrations, and obtain information on the experiences of others in procuring systems. Readers of the business case will need to be assured that the market is sufficiently buoyant and active to make the proposal worth pursuing.

4 Options

Readers of the business case are bound to ask what options there are, other than introducing electronic records management.

- *Do nothing* – the preceding analysis of context, drivers, current state of electronic records management and best practice will need to be brought to bear in discussing the option of staying with paper records in managing information or, if it is the case, of continuing to operate a local area network. For example, in the UK public sector a significant driver has been the 'Modernising Government' agenda, whereby targets have been set by government to deliver services to the public online, to manage government information electronically and to provide greater access to government information. In the private sector the driving forces are often the advantage of sharing information, collaborative working or perhaps pressure on costs. What will be the effect on your organization if you continue to manage your records in the same way as now while other similar organizations are introducing electronic systems? Will it make working with them or other stakeholders more difficult? An important consideration in discussing this option is how aware readers will be of it. Rather than bombard them with detail – most of which they are likely to know – a good approach will be to present a broad outline and be prepared to answer any questions later.
- *Interim solution* – someone may suggest not going the whole way with electronic records management but introducing a phased approach. For example, a current IT infrastructure could be modified to take an electronic document management

system or enterprise content management system that is effective in managing current records but lacks the functionalities relating to disposal. Although the reduction of costs may be a motive, the argument for interim solutions or phased approaches is often based on the importance of culture change and thus the need for a gradual evolution of working practices that rely on electronic rather than paper records. Whether such interim solutions are viable in your organization will depend very much on the situation in which you find yourself. In some cases they may be viable while in others past experience may be relevant. If you are convinced that an interim solution will not work, clearly you will need to be well prepared to argue your case.

5 Requirements

So much work has been done on functional requirements for electronic records management systems that it would be pointless to try and repeat it here. Before citing links to useful material, however, it might be worthwhile to make a few general remarks on this aspect of the business case.

While all electronic records management systems need to meet several generic requirements, each organization will always have to consider its own business needs and context when drawing up its specifications. The broad areas of generic requirements that all systems ought to meet (often referred to as the 'core requirements') are:

- declaring an electronic document to be a corporate record
- maintaining the record as reliable and authentic evidence of a business action or decision
- building and managing a file plan so that files and folders can be classified
- managing the metadata of the records
- managing the retention and disposal of records
- searching for and retrieving records
- controlling access to records.

You can see that these core requirements relate closely to the underlying principles of records management examined in Chapter 1.

You will often hear the need for a structured file plan called into question. Why, with such effective search mechanisms, can we not just save all electronic documents in one area? This has some merit but it is a very short-term view. Records need to be organized to facilitate the management of a group of related records as a single unit for the purposes of scheduling, review, preservation and destruction, so that a management process can be applied reliably to records in the group at the same time. Evidential use of the records (any records) is based on functions. Users beyond immediate business needs usually want all documents relating to a specific subject or function. The structure reflects and supports the business activities and corporate objectives of an organization. In the longer term this is most definitely the case; researchers are looking at assemblies of records, not simply individual documents. In addition, the disposal of unwanted material is more effectively undertaken if the file plan has a functional structure of related records in files and folders.

Currently, and for a few more years yet, the subject of hybrid records needs to be taken into account. Hybrid records are here defined as those records that are on the same subject, project or case but which are in a mixture of forms, usually paper and electronic. They become particularly difficult to manage at the appraisal and disposal stages because of the different timescales that have traditionally been applied. Hybrid records management is examined in more detail in Chapter 10.

There are two main sources for examining electronic records management requirements and for drawing up your own specifications:

- *MoReq2*: these **Mo**del **Req**uirements for the management of electronic records are the result of a project undertaken by the DLM Forum (DLM is an acronym for the French *données lisibles par machine*, in English: 'machine readable data'), a body set up in 1994 for the promotion of greater co-operation in the field of archives. See www.cornwell.co.uk/edrm/moreq.asp.
- *The UK National Archives* has published *Requirements for Electronic Records Management Systems*, which comprises four parts:
  — functional requirements
  — metadata standard
  — reference document
  — implementation guide.
  See www.nationalarchives.gov.uk/electronicrecords/reqs2002/default.htm.

6 Benefits

This is probably the most important part of the business case. Most decision makers on projects such as this will have benefits uppermost in their minds. They will, of course, be closely linked with costs. If the organization spends this large amount of money, how will it benefit?

The basic purpose of this part of the business case is to confirm that the expected benefits outweigh the expected investment and the expected risks.

The examination of benefits does not stop at identification. It must also include support for the achievement of the identified benefits and their evaluation and measurement. These aspects are covered under the subject of change management in Chapter 13.

Planning benefits

Part of the governance of electronic records management projects should include benefits management. One person should be responsible for this particular area of work. Planning for the identification of benefits should include:

- agreeing on the benefits which will be measured
- drawing up a benefits register (see example at the end of this chapter)
- determining who is responsible for the delivery and measurement of each identified benefit
- ensuring that stakeholders are aware of and committed to effective delivery of the benefits.

Categorizing benefits

It is useful to categorize benefits so that common factors of measurement can be applied. The following breakdown covers the key areas:

- *Financial* – financial benefits are those that can be measured in monetary terms (such as savings in licence fees for systems that have been replaced) or in terms that can be translated into monetary value (such as staff time). Indeed staff time often accounts for a large part of the financial justification for electronic records management. Sometimes, however, the result is that the time saved is used on different work and therefore becomes a stakeholder benefit (see below) rather than a financial one. Some examples of financial benefits are:
  — saving in time to file information – no longer need to print out documents, find the correct file, insert the documents and index them
  — saving in time to retrieve information – including searching for and accessing files, waiting for files in use by somebody else, and any photocopying
  — saving in re-work time when previous work cannot be found
  — reduced storage space in desks, filing cabinets and cupboards, and also in intermediate storage (often through a data storage company)
  — long-term reduction in the requirement for paper
  — reduction in the need to purchase consumables, such as file covers, printer cartridges, etc.
  Financial savings are usually important at the corporate level but may not be a good motivator at a local level because of the fear that budget cuts will result.
- *Stakeholder* – essentially these are benefits experienced by people. The majority of these will be staff who will benefit as a result of the new system or process changes that might be implemented. The benefits are measured by staff surveys where questions about perception of matters such as ease of filing, access to information and ability to respond quickly can be scored. They may also include people with whom the organization has regular dealings, such as other government departments or subsidiary companies. Although these

measures cannot be precise, this is a useful way of interpreting some of the more intangible benefits. Some examples of staff benefits are:
— better quality work and (thus) improved morale
— ready access to information which staff need to do their job
— opportunity for more flexible work patterns (such as home working).
- *Business* – these are closely related to stakeholder benefits but are more aligned with corporate business plans and key performance indicators. When describing this type of benefit it may be useful to define business at a local level. In this way the benefits provide a focal point for local teams to evaluate and demonstrate the improvements which the use of an electronic records management system is making to issues that are an important part of operational activities. There are many examples of benefits in this category, such as:
— awareness and use of information available elsewhere may achieve reductions in reworking
— retention of knowledge when staff leave or retire is improved
— linking the electronic records management system to internet/intranet content management systems enables information aimed at the public and staff to be updated and maintained more effectively
— there is immediate access to documents as soon as they are filed
— the ability to share documents easily with colleagues is enhanced
— knowledge sharing is promoted
— accessibility of material outside normal hours enables staff to respond to urgent business requirements
— there is greater ability to search for documents under several parameters (e.g. keyword, author), thus making the records much more useful
— the planning process is assisted through the better management of information on the records management system itself
— responses to enquiries are made more effective (for example under freedom of information and data protection) through managing information corporately
— there are back-up copies of vital records in the event of a disaster
— there is reliable evidence for accountability and auditability
— there is better security and confidentiality of information since these are more explicitly managed.

Identifying benefits

What is the best way of identifying potential benefits and assigning responsibility for them? Inevitably this is likely to be a very labour-intensive exercise but the spin-offs from it (such as a greater awareness of electronic records management, local 'buy-in', etc.) can be beneficial themselves. It is often useful to run workshops with local teams to identify performance benefits that can then be measured and tracked during the implementation of electronic records management. These workshops could cover corporate objectives as well as local ones.

7 Governance

The business case needs to describe how a large project like planning and implementing electronic records management will be managed. It needs, for example, to identify what the critical success factors of the project will be. These will be centred largely round the realization of the benefits described above but they will also include timing and cost of the project itself.

A critical skill in any project is the management of change. This includes identifying and taking into consideration the point of view of all project stakeholders; identifying and minimizing points of resistance; evaluating and countering risks; assessing and encouraging people's willingness to change; and evaluating the process of change. How this is managed is examined in detail in Chapter 13.

Project management

Key stages in the management of projects are:

- planning the project
- analysing the organization
- designing solutions
- implementing the design
- evaluating the results.

There are several methodologies available for the management of projects of all kinds. One commonly used in the public sector in the UK and widely recognized in the UK private sector is PRINCE 2 (**PR**ojects **IN** Controlled Environments), which was first established in 1989. The key features of the methodology are:

- its focus on business justification
- a defined organization structure for the project management team
- its product-based planning approach
- its emphasis on dividing the project into manageable and controllable stages
- its flexibility to be applied at a level appropriate to the project.

For more information on this particular methodology see www.ogc.gov.uk/methods_prince_2.asp.

Key features of a project

- *Aims and objectives*. Once the issue is identified (in this case the planning and implementation of electronic records management), the project's aims and objectives need to be defined. It is essential to consult with stakeholders in order to formulate a coherent set of aims and objectives. These must, of course, also support the organization's overall corporate IT strategy and its general vision and purpose. For example, they might be framed as follows:

— design and implement a corporate electronic records management system that supports [*the organization's*] business plans and objectives

— ensure that the project is in accordance with, and meets the objectives of, e-government policy [*or similar sector policy*]

— ensure that the selected electronic records management system complies with relevant standards, such as ISO 15489, ISO 17799, PD 0008 and XML

— introduce new working practices for the management of the organization's records and information

— manage the change processes required to implement the selected electronic records management system.

• *Project scope*. Defining the scope of the project is important. Projects can quickly become unmanageable if their scope is defined too broadly, and they can be ineffective if their scope is too narrow. Defining the project scope entails assessing the feasibility and likelihood of successfully realizing the broad project objectives. To arrive at the project's appropriate scope, it is necessary to refine the broad project objectives to ensure a greater likelihood of success.

The scope of a project to implement electronic records management is likely to include the development of accompanying policies and procedures (they will almost certainly change as a result of moving from a paper to an electronic environment). It may also need to include closely related functions in the organization, such as freedom of information or data protection. The most important aspect of it, however, is that it has to be corporate. All electronic records management systems, almost by definition, are corporate undertakings.

• *Project deliverables*. Having determined the project's objectives and scope, the next step is to identify its deliverables. Clearly the main deliverable in our electronic records management project is a fully functional system. There will, of course, be several other products and they will include some or all of the following:

— new records management policy statement

— appraisal policy and procedures for electronic records

— set of procedures for the creation and management of corporate information

— training programme for all staff

— performance management scheme to measure the effectiveness of the new system.

• *Project personnel*. It is extremely unlikely that a project of this nature will be undertaken by one person (unless you have a miniscule organization). A team of people with the requisite skills and knowledge should manage the project. The organization's stakeholders should be strongly represented. Moreover, when the scope of the project is likely to result in the redesign of business processes, wide-scale input and involvement is critical in order to reduce any resistance to organizational change. Thus, establishing a temporary organizational

structure is an important part of project planning. A typical structure (in line with the PRINCE 2 methodology mentioned above) will consist of
— project manager
— business, technical and user representatives
— team administration
— steering committee.
Each of the roles should be defined.

While this represents a model organizational structure for a project, such a formal and complex structure may be neither necessary nor possible. It should be adapted to suit the scope and objectives, the available resources (human and financial) and the organizational context of the project.

• *Communication.* Yet another essential part of project management is the communications plan. So many projects falter because of lack of communication between participants and/or stakeholders. The recipients of information about the progress of the project or the delivery of its products should be clearly defined and a specific project team member assigned responsibility for carrying out the agreed method of communication. As much use as possible should be made of newsletters, intranets, sectional meetings, etc. The plan can take the form of a simple table (see Table 3.1).

Table 3.1 Communications plan

Audience	Information	Owner	Frequency	Method
IT strategy team	Progress on procurement; Risks and issues; Development of revised policy documents	Project manager	Every 3 months	Meeting and e-mail
Management Board	Progress	Project manager	Every 3 months	Highlight report
Internal staff	Project scope and objectives; Training plans; Progress	Assigned project team member	Monthly	Intranet and newsletters
				etc.

• *Quality.* The project should include a quality plan. The person generally responsible for ensuring the quality of deliverables would be the project manager. In a major undertaking like the implementation of electronic records management this can be a major aspect. The main deliverable – the system itself – will need to go through a strict testing programme. Changes resulting from this programme will need to be raised with the project board and approved by them before being raised as a formal request for change with the installation personnel. In addition to these controls the project board ought to include a project assurance co-ordinator to provide independent quality assurance (see

the description of PRINCE 2 for further information).
* *Documentation.* Project governance should be supported by the appropriate documentation. This should comprise:
  — project initiation document (PID)
  — project plan
  — risk register
  — issues log
  — reports.

The key features described above should be set out in a project initiation document (PID). This is what describes the project, providing some background and defining the objectives, scope, deliverables, resources and governance. It will include such items as the communication and quality plans described above.

The project plan should break the project down into achievable pieces of work and show the timescales for each. An effective way of showing the plan in the UK has frequently been the use of Gantt charts, an example of which follows at the end of this chapter.

The Risk Register contains a description of the risks to the project that have been identified and proposals for managing them. It should include a scheme for rating the degree of risk (see Chapter 11). An example of a risk register is shown at the end of this chapter.

The Issues Log is a record of all the issues that arise during the course of the project and the decisions made on how to manage them. An example of an issues log is shown at the end of this chapter.

The project should make formal reports to stakeholders and other interested parties. Most of these reports will be specified in the communications plan (for example, highlight reports).

Evaluation

This governance section of the business plan ought to state explicitly that evaluation and measurement of the project will take place. In many large projects of this nature there are staged evaluations and key indicators are used to measure performance. For example, there might be evaluations at each design stage (see Chapter 4) and at each roll-out of the electronic records management system. All projects ought to have a post implementation review – often called a 'lessons learnt' exercise.

A very effective device for evaluation can be a sector-based forum. In the UK central government sector, for example, a Post-Implementation Forum was set up in 2005 and the group has held workshops at which attendees have been able to share and learn from each others' experiences on designing and planning electronic records management systems. Participants share their experiences, good and bad, and highlight any significant issues that have arisen during their implementation programme. For example, the first meeting of this particular forum emphasized the need for detailed planning, effective change management and high-quality training.

8 Costs

By this stage you will have provided the context for electronic records management, given an assessment of the current situation in the organization and explained how electronic records management systems operate. You will also have provided the framework for undertaking the proposed project and described the benefits that are likely to be realized from the introduction of a new system. All these factors now need to be brought together into that part of the business case in which most senior managers will be interested and on which many of them will base their judgement of the viability of the project. It hardly needs saying that the analysis of costs of the enterprise must be accurate and able to be justified.

Presenting readers with a mass of figures can detract from the effectiveness of the business case. It might be better if a broad outline or summaries of the costs are made and the detailed figures are presented in an annex. While your organization may have a corporate template for presenting costs, the following framework (Table 3.2) may be a useful guide to how they might be presented:

Table 3.2 Summary of costs

Description	Year 1 £	Year 2 £	Total £
Planning and implementation of ERM			
Procurement and project support (consultancy)			
Hardware and software			
Technical support			
Administration			
Implementation			
Running costs (including licences)			
User costs			
Migration			
SUB-TOTAL			
Business and culture change			
Development/revision of policies			
Change management			
Training			
Communications			
SUB-TOTAL			
TOTAL			

Breakdown of costs

Procurement

- Standard Catalogue Investigations
- Official Journal of the European Communities (OJEC)

Support

- Management

- Consultancy

Hardware

- Server
- Index server
- Scanners
- Systems back up
- PC upgrades
- Installation
- Operations training

Software

- ERM system
- Scanning
- Back up
- Operating system
- E-mail interface

Technical support

- ICT Staff
- Operational training

Administration

- Training
- Office support
- Project team

Implementation

- Network
- Services
- Accommodation
- Policies and standards
- Design and analysis
- Development
- Testing
- Piloting
- Change management
- Roll out

Running costs

- Accommodation services
- Network
- Maintenance – hardware and software
- Licences
- Consumables (paper, tapes, etc.)
- Staffing

User costs
- Training – ERM, scanning, records management support groups, etc.
- Lost time (through training on new systems, etc.)

Migration
- Data migration (paper and electronic)
- Write-offs.

When gathering information about these costs you will acquire lots of information, perhaps in both paper and electronic form. All this needs to be kept at least for the lifetime of the project. It will, of course, be needed to justify any of the figures that you have put forward in the business case. Great care should be taken in marshalling this information. It requires your best records management skills to make it accessible! Indeed this might be said for all the documentation acquired as a result of the project.

An important element of the costs of a project of this nature is the analysis that needs to be made over its whole life. How long this might be depends on many factors – size of the organization, scope of the project, available expertise, funding, to name but a few. Cost benefit analysis is a relatively simple technique for deciding whether it is economical to make a change. It requires adding up the value of the benefits that have been identified (although that identification may not be easy or exact in many cases, especially for those intangible benefits that were described earlier) and subtracting from the total the costs of the proposed course of action. Some projects opt for an analysis of financial costs only, simply because it is so difficult to forecast intangible benefits and costs.

However, you will also need to undertake a discounted cash flow analysis. This technique takes into account the time value of money. As we know only too well, over time the value of the same amount of money changes. For example, if you were offered £100 today or £100 in a year's time, you would be better off to take the £100 today. Because of inflation the £100 will buy you more now than in a year's time. [There is, of course, also the possibility that you might want to invest the £100 and earn interest on it, in which case it will be worth more than £100 in a year's time]. This is the basis for discounted cash flow and it will allow you to analyse the costs of a project more accurately.

9 Conclusion

It is always useful to have a conclusion to the business case – bringing together any important points and, in as brief a way as possible, summarizing the main points of the case. For example:

The implementation of an electronic records management system offers a significant opportunity for [*the organization*]. As well as modernizing its approach to the management of information generally, it will promote the better and easier accessibility of information to enable [*the organization*] to undertake its work more efficiently and to meet all its legislative and regulatory requirements.

10 Annexes

Readers of the business case will generally want to examine significant issues relating to the proposed project and be satisfied that all the relevant points have been covered. They will not want to be confronted with masses of detail as part of the main narrative. That detail, however, needs to be included in the business case as evidence and the best place for it is as an annex or annexes to the report. This will provide a simple way for the reader to examine the detail if they are so inclined. Annexes might cover:

- descriptions of ERM systems
- detailed requirements
- benefits descriptions and analysis
- detailed costs.

APPENDIX
Model business case annexes

Table A3.1 Example benefits register

No.	Benefit	Description	Critical level (1–5)	Metric	Expected outcome	Baseline	Measure-ment interval	Person responsible
Category								
1	Information retrieval time	Time spent searching for and retrieving required information from the ERM system	2	Survey users on the average time spent retrieving required information	Decrease	1) from current paper system 2) from ERM system as soon as imple-mented	Project end	
2	Reduction in storage space	Reduction of filing of paper on paper files and folders, and space required to store files	2	1) Accommodation space 2) Accommodation costs 3) Number of file covers issued	Decrease	Amount of storage space at project end	Yearly	
3	Improvement in business processes	Current business procedures and improvements in time and quality	3	Stakeholder survey	Less time spent on procedural work; better decision making	From initial functional analysis		

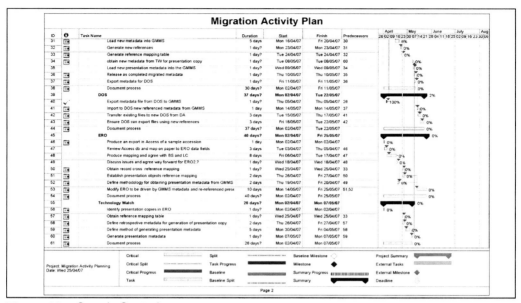

Figure A3.1 Sample Gantt chart
Reproduced with kind permission from The National Archives

Table A3.2 Sample risk register

Ref.	Description	Category	Impact (1–3)	Probability (1–3)	Lack of control (1–3)	Proximity (1–3)	Risk rating	Countermeasures	Owner	Contingency plans	Date entered	Updated	Status
2	Lack of resources – budgets	2	3	2	2	24	Cost modelling. Resource planning. Budget planning.	KJS	Seek more funding. If necessary, amend scope and task timetables	29/5	15/1	open
3	Lack of resources – manpower, skills	3	2	2	2	24	Resource planning. Budget planning.	KJS	Seek more resources	29/5	15/1	open
7	Lack of co-ordinated communications plan	3	3	2	2	36	Compile plan	GG	Use process team leader forum to encourage teams to produce individual plans	19/9	22/1	open
9	No formal project manager	3	3	2	3	54		DB	Management Board agreed to appoint	7/7	16/11	closed

Table A3.3 Sample issues log

No.	Description	Rating (H, M, L)	Type	Owner	Author	Actions	Date identified	Date last updated	Current status	Reference number
9	How do we get departmental buy-in?	M		MS	JS	Open Day held with positive feedback. Communications sent to departments. Advice posted on organization's intranet. KJS to speak to series of monthly departmental meetings. Further workshops planned in coming twelve months.	9/11	3/1	open	
10	Organizational change due to need for specialized staff	H		IH	JS	To be addressed by change management project. HD appointed to represent stakeholders.	15/10	30/10	open	

Part 2

Design

Main issues for design

This chapter examines the three main issues that will affect the design of your electronic records management system: requirements, metadata and policy.

Before embarking on a general discussion of development of the requirements, it may be useful to describe the different systems that are available and which, for the purposes of this book, are described as 'electronic records management systems'.

For several years we have had *electronic document management* (EDM) systems. These help organizations to provide better access to information and in particular to support workflow arrangements typically undertaken by team working. They also enable organizations to exploit their information resources more effectively – it is difficult to imagine how we could have provided the same level of information with paper systems as we do now with such electronic systems. EDM generally supports immediate business needs and does not embrace all records management functions (e.g. disposal). It will usually only handle information at the document level. It typically provides for:

- storage of records
- version control
- indexing
- search and retrieval
- access control
- ability to archive offline
- audit
- interface with other systems such as workflow and document image processing.

Electronic records management (ERM) systems add standard records management practices to EDM. These include a corporate filing structure and disposal scheduling.

The requirements would typically include the following, in addition to those provided by an EDM system:

- management of information as corporate information (including the ability to declare records corporate as and when required)
- storage, indexing, search and retrieval of all types of records and documents
- management of information in a way that maintains links between records
- record level metadata describing contextual information
- management of hybrid records
- authentication of information
- support for legal and regulatory requirements
- appraisal and disposal of records
- export of records for permanent preservation.

Electronic document and records management (EDRM) systems are largely exactly what they say. EDM systems have been extending their functionality to include specialist packages that are common in ERM systems. The result is an integrated system.

Enterprise content management (ECM) or content management systems (CMS) are the terms now used for systems that in recent times were called ERM or EDRM. However, you will have an idea of how imprecise the term still is when you find definitions that begin 'ECM is a broad term that means many different things to many different people . . .' (Google, April 2007). Typically the term is understood to mean any strategy or technology for managing the capture, storage, retrieval, distribution, security, preservation and destruction of documents and content. It embraces most, if not all, of the functionality described in EDM, ERM and EDRM above. ECM systems are designed to manage both structured and unstructured content. They combine a wide variety of technologies and components, some of which are often used as stand-alone systems. For our purposes we might consider the term as one that is gradually replacing ERM and as one that covers systems that attempt to manage all our information, be it in our corporate folders, on our intranet, in e-mail systems or on web pages.

Requirements

The business case – discussed in Chapter 3 – will need to make some general remarks about the requirements of an electronic records management system. A broad outline of these will suffice in that context, but once approval is given to proceed with a project, the design stage will need to specify in detail what the requirements are for the system you wish to implement. You may wish to use one of the generic requirement documents that are available (for example, MoReq and The National Archives, as highlighted in Chapter 3). More likely, you will wish to use these as a basis for drawing up your own particular requirements, since this consideration of requirements for your electronic records management system must lead to a full specification that can be costed and bid for by potential suppliers. Clearly, an organization will have its own specialist needs and will be approaching the implementation of electronic records management from a particular existing situation in which no other, or very few, organizations will find themselves. There will always be a need to tailor generic requirements. This might include:

- selecting alternative requirements that are more in accordance with the organization's corporate policy and procedures
- adding specialist needs
- prioritizing requirements, typically by tagging them as *mandatory*, *highly desirable* or *desirable*.

How do you know what requirements your organization will want for an electronic records management system? The key to this is to know what the current record keeping situation is and what managers and other staff want out of a system. Clearly there has to be substantial dialogue here; the managers and staff will not know what they want until they are aware of what an electronic records management system is capable of. Will these capabilities fit into the corporate structure or corporate culture? The dialogue, of course, has to include technical staff, but the design of the system must be based on good records management principles. Identifying your requirements is akin to undertaking a records audit or information survey. This procedure is examined in detail in Chapter 5.

The requirements document that you create must be exactly what you and your organization want. That may sound obvious, but there is often the temptation to be persuaded by software companies to say you want what they think you want. You want the system to adapt to your needs and requirements, not the other way round. At the design stage the floor is yours – this is the opportunity to specify all those activities and procedures in managing your records and information whose absence you and your colleagues have bemoaned for years. A clean slate – what more can you wish?

You will need to specify two types of requirements – functional and non-functional. The former cover the operation of the system itself, such as:

- declaration of records as corporate records – the ability to make or create a record
- classification (the file plan) – the ability to classify and group like records together
- sustainability – the ability to maintain a record
- retention and disposal – the ability to set out disposal schedules and to put them into effect
- access management – the ability to control access to the records
- authentication – the ability to manage records to the standards necessary for compliance with requirements for legal admissibility and to demonstrate that compliance

- audit – the ability to record an audit trail of events within the system
- managing hybrid records – the ability to support the management and integration of information about paper records
- importing information and records from other systems (e.g. databases) – the ability to import bulk records and structures without degradation of content or format
- advanced records retrieval – the ability to retrieve records and folders to a specified standard.

The latter cover the environment in which the system operates, such as:

- ease of use
- scalability
- performance
- maintainability
- standards
- documentation
- training and consultancy.

One seemingly minor but nonetheless important aspect of the statement of requirements is the use of terminology. In such a document there must be no ambiguity. Suppliers must be in no doubt about what you want your system to do. The use of words like 'should' and 'must' must be carefully chosen to reflect your requirements.

Metadata

Much has been written about metadata in electronic records management systems. Most of it is bound up in technical language and frameworks. This section is intended to provide a basic understanding of the subject – enough to be able to work with the technical experts to provide acceptable solutions.

Paper environment

We had/have metadata in the paper environment but we may not have recognized it or called it by that name. We have tended and tend now to call it 'documentation'. The documentation of the appraisal of records has always been a particularly important aspect of records management. It has promoted consistency in the retention of records and in their selection for permanent preservation. In addition, in recent years the documentation of record keeping in general has become a vital component of records management systems. For example, the move towards greater openness in government and the introduction of freedom of information legislation have given the documentation of records work an extra significance.

Information described in Table 4.1 has generally been recommended for documenting paper records management systems.

Table 4.1 Documenting paper records management systems

Item	Description
Series identifier	This will usually consist of a title, and an alphabetical or alpha-numeric prefix (e.g. Financial Policy series, 2/FIN)
Format and structure	This should include the physical nature of the series or collection (e.g. computer files, registered paper files, microfiche) and a description of the filing system (hierarchical, co-ordinated theme, numerical, etc.)
Index/finding aid	The method by which access to the series or collection is given should be recorded. This might be a computer database or a simple card index
Time span	The start and end dates of the series, and of individual records, should be recorded (the time span of series might be different from that of individual records)
Subject matter	This should include the purpose for which the records were collected or created, such as reference to any relevant legislation
Creators	The department, division or unit which created the records
Users	The departments, divisions or units which had access to the records and used them in the course of their work
Related records	This should include earlier and later series of records
Disposal	A record of the appraisal criteria applied, including references to the relevant acquisition or collections policy, and any correspondence between the Records Manager and the archive should be kept. This should also include any disposal schedule for the series or collection
Access	Any restrictions on the information contained in the series, either under legislative provisions or sensitivity criteria, should be recorded (protective marking)
Transferred records	Information about records transferred, migrated or separated from the series (for example, as a result of a change in functions) and about any records that have been re-registered in the series should also be recorded.

Electronic environment

The term 'metadata' is used differently in different communities. Some use it to refer to machine-understandable information while others use it only for records that describe electronic resources. Metadata is commonly used for any formal scheme of resource description, applying it to any type of object. For example, metadata schemes have been developed to describe published books, archival finding aids, art objects and educational materials as well as electronic records. Numerous standard schemes have been developed to address specific information use and management needs. These standards have emerged from the needs of specific interest groups to standardize how they classify information.

There are four main types of metadata:

• Descriptive metadata describes a resource for purposes such as discovery and

identification such as title, author and keywords
- Structural metadata shows how compound objects are put together: for example, how pages are ordered in a report or a book to form sections or chapters
- Administrative metadata provides information to manage a resource – for example, when and how it was created, file type and other technical information, and who can access it
- Preservation metadata contains information needed to archive and preserve a resource.

Metadata can be embedded into an electronic record/digital object or it can be stored separately. Storing it with the object it describes ensures that it will not be lost, helps ensure that both will be updated together and may avoid some of the problems that might be encountered by links between metadata and object. On the other hand, storing metadata separately can simplify its management and make search and retrieval easier. It is now common practice to store metadata in a database system and link it to the documents it describes.

Most metadata work concentrates on the tracking of recently created resources. However, because concern is increasing that electronic resources may not survive for long periods and various preservation strategies are being examined and implemented (see Chapter 8), it has become key to ensuring that resources will survive and continue to be accessible into the future. Emulation, for example, requires special elements to record where an electronic record came from, how it has changed over time and what characteristics it possesses.

Many metadata schemes have been developed for a variety of environments. Among the most common in the records and information areas are:

1 Dublin Core – originating from a workshop held in Dublin, Ohio, in 1995, this scheme's objective was to define a set of elements that could be used by authors to describe their own world wide web resources. This was a time when there was a great proliferation of electronic resources that the library profession found impossible to catalogue; the aim of members of the workshop was therefore to define a few elements and some simple rules that could be used. There are 15 elements:
   — Title
   — Creator
   — Subject
   — Description
   — Publisher
   — Contributor
   — Date
   — Type
   — Format
   — Identifier

— Source
— Language
— Relation
— Coverage
— Rights.

Because of its simplicity the Dublin Core set is used by many outside the library community and used in many other types of materials and applications than web-based documents. Over the years there has been much debate over semantics and enlarging the number of elements but the scheme has continued to take a minimalist view.

2 Metadata Encoding and Transmission Standard (METS) – developed as a standard data structure for describing complex electronic library objects and packaging descriptive, structural and administrative metadata together.

3 Encoded Archival Description (EAD) – a way of marking up the data in finding aids so that they can be searched and displayed online. It is particularly popular in academic libraries, large record repositories and museums where large collections of unique material have not been individually catalogued like traditional library materials.

4 MARC 21 – defines a data format that provides the mechanism by which computers exchange, use and interpret bibliographic information; its data elements make up the foundation of most library catalogues, particularly in the United States of America. MARC is an acronym for **MA**chine **R**eadable Cataloguing.

5 ISAD(G) – the General International Standard Archival Description, a standard that provides general guidance for the preparation of archival descriptions. It is generally used in conjunction with existing national standards and contains rules for archival description that can be applied irrespective of the form or medium of the archival material.

Many metadata creation tools have been developed. These have generally been introduced to support specific metadata schemes or element sets. The websites for the particular scheme usually have links to relevant tools. They are of four types:

1 *Templates*, which allow the user to enter metadata values into pre-set fields that match the element set being used. The template then generates a formatted set of attributes.

2 *Mark-up tools*, which structure metadata attributes into a specified language – usually XML or SGML.

3 *Extraction tools*, which automatically create metadata from an analysis of the electronic resource.

4 *Conversion tools*, which translate one metadata format to another.

Mention should be made of the e-Government Metadata Standard (e-GMS).

This describes in detail the way that metadata should be structured and lists the elements and refinements that should be used by the UK public sector to create metadata for information resources. It also gives guidance on the purpose and use of each element.

Policy statement

The requirements document that you draw up should include a copy of your organization's records management policy statement. In many instances the basic document (a model for which is shown in the Appendix at the end of Chapter 1) has been adapted to reflect the management of electronic records. Such a policy should set out integrated principles for electronic records management in existing and new systems to guide procedures and practices, and thus provide a solid platform for incorporating the general principles of electronic records management into day-to-day operations.

An ERM policy statement (a model of which is included at the end of this chapter) should contain the following elements:

- purpose
- scope
- requirements (records, system and process)
- relationship with other policies
- access
- security
- preservation
- policy review.

It is debatable, of course, what you call an integrated policy statement like the model. Is it just a records management policy or an electronic records management policy? Increasingly we are moving towards managing all our information electronically and we might therefore adopt the former descriptor. Even at present most of us are managing our paper records electronically in that we have databases or spreadsheets that serve as finding aids to the records, although we may still be using the record itself in paper form.

Purpose

The purpose of the policy is to:

- define the scope of records management
- provide clear guidance on why records need to be kept
- explain how good records management serves the needs of the organization
- define responsibilities for the management of records

• set out principles and policies from which procedures can be implemented.

Scope

The policy should aim to cover all records – paper, electronic and other media – and those records that will be created in the future. It should cover the requirements that need to be met for the records to be considered as a proper corporate record of the organization and the requirements for systems and processes that deal with the records (especially, in an electronic context, their quality, authenticity and reliability). The policy should cover the key issues of access, security and preservation, which take on added importance with electronic records management. It should be integrated with the organization's overall strategy and mission, and be reviewed on a regular basis.

Requirements

The information generated by the organization must be managed so that it forms a proper corporate record. The basic requirements for this must be:

• the record is present
• the record is accessible
• the record can be interpreted
• the record can be trusted
• the record can be maintained
• the record is documented.

Systems and processes need to be managed so that these record requirements are met. These need to make available records for classification, transfer or disposal in accordance with the general records management principles. They need to keep the records secure and ensure that they are maintained in such a way that they are available for as long as the organization needs them. The systems must also have regard to legal and other regulatory requirements (for example, Freedom of Information, Data Protection, copyright, international standards). The processes should also include the provision of management information on the records.

Relationship with other policies

If the records management policy is to be effective, it must be stated explicitly within it how records management fits in with other strategies and policies. In the electronic records management context the crucial integration must be with the organization's information and communications technology (ICT) strategy. The management of electronic records will, of course, not only depend on the support of technical staff but on the resources and backing that that function receives in the organization. It can also work the other way round – it is often evident that the records management policy itself, when integrated with the organization's vision, can provide the framework and requirements for the necessary ICT processes and procedures to be in place to deliver on the vision. Other policies with which records management needs to be integrated include access to/freedom of information, protection of personal data and audit.

Access

Policy on access is required to ensure that the movement of information in and out of the records management system is controlled, so that the records can be seen by different categories of users. It is likely that certain types of records (for example, personnel, finance) or their content (for example, names of individuals in reports, minutes of particular meetings) should only be accessible by certain people in the organization. In addition some information may be restricted by policies on copyright, data protection or other regulations. There may also be both internal and external considerations as far as access is concerned. The question of access is examined more closely in Chapter 9.

Security

Policy on security should seek not only to protect the records themselves but also the records management infrastructure. Only in this way will users be confident in the management of electronic records. When implementing electronic records management systems this is often a major stumbling block. However much computers have become a common part of our lives, there is still some mistrust about them. Can we be confident that they (or the systems that run them) will protect confidential information? The basis for assuring our colleagues that this is the case is here. Time spent on security policy and procedures is time well spent.

Preservation

The sustainability of information is a key issue in an electronic records management environment. We have become used to storing information (in paper form) in a records centre or archive and being sure that it will still be there, and accessible, in 20, 50 or more years later. This will not be the case with electronic records. Technology changes frequently. New software and new versions of existing software are regularly introduced so that we can manage our information ever more effectively and efficiently. The preservation part of the policy should seek to minimize the risks associated with technological changes and ensure that those records that are needed remain intact. It should also take account of non-technical changes, such as organizational and business changes. This important aspect of preservation is examined in more detail in Chapter 8.

Policy review

It is no good having a well structured and comprehensive records management policy if people in the organization are unaware of it. As well as being reviewed to ensure that it is up to date, the policy should also be reviewed to see how well (or how badly) it is being adhered to in the organization. The review should include recommended remedial action, if any is required.

APPENDIX
Model (Electronic) Records and Information Management Policy Statement

Purpose

Information is a corporate asset and the records of [*the organization*] are important sources of administrative, fiscal, legal, evidential and historical information. They are vital to the organization in its current and future operations, for the purposes of accountability, and for an awareness and understanding of its history. They are the corporate memory of the organization.

This policy provides a framework for the management of records and information in [*the organization*]. Its purpose is to provide clear guidance on why we need to keep records and on how they should be managed in accordance with [*the organization's*] overall vision and business strategy. It defines the scope of records management, the responsibilities for discharging the function effectively and aims to set out the principles from which procedures can be implemented.

Scope

This policy provides for:

- the requirements that must be met for the records of [*the organization*] to be considered as a proper record of the activity of the organization
- the requirements for systems and processes that deal with records
- the quality and reliability which must be maintained to provide a valuable information and knowledge resource for the organization
- review of the policy and checking the quality of implementation
- an overall statement of records management policy which is supplemented by detailed procedures.

It covers records in all formats, created in the course of [*the organization's*] business.

Requirements
Records requirements

Records must be created to record accurately the business activities and transactions of the organization, they must be able to be stored and maintained for as long as required by the organization and they must be destroyed or transferred to other organizations for permanent preservation when no longer required for operational purposes. [*The organization*] will endeavour at all times to ensure that:

- *The record is present*. The information required to undertake the management and operational activities of the organization is properly recorded
- *The record is accessible*. It is possible to locate and retrieve information and deliver it in a way that is true to the original record to those who need to make use of it
- *The record can be interpreted*. The information is in context, so that it can be shown when and where it was created, who created it, how it was used and how it relates to other information
- *The record can be trusted*. The information exactly matches that which was created and used, and its authenticity and integrity can be demonstrated beyond reasonable doubt
- *The record can be maintained*. The information can be accessed, used and trusted for as long as required, even when transferred to another location or system, and any sensitive information is kept securely in accordance with relevant standards
- *The record is documented*. Suitable documentation on the organization's records and information is available so that the system can be managed effectively and decisions taken on its resource requirements.

Legislative requirements

In consultation with organizations which may be concerned with the management of its records, [*the organization*] will create, use, manage and destroy or preserve its records in accordance with all statutory requirements.

Roles and responsibilities

All staff of [*the organization*] that create, use, manage or dispose of records have a duty to protect them and to ensure that any information that they add to the record is accurate, complete and necessary. All staff involved in managing records will receive the necessary training.

The *Chief Executive* has a duty to ensure that [*the organization*] complies with the requirements of legislation affecting management of the records, and with supporting regulations and codes.

The *Records Manager* will work closely with Heads of Departments to ensure that there is consistency in the management of records and that advice and guidance on good records management practice is provided.

Managerial and technical staff are responsible for ensuring that records and information systems in their areas conform to this policy and to the requirements of legislation.

All members of staff are responsible for documenting their actions and decisions in the records and for maintaining the records in accordance with good records management practice.

Relationship with other policies

Maintaining the effectiveness of this policy means that it must integrate with other corporate policies and standards. These include:

- vision/mission statement
- information and communication technology (ICT) strategy
- records and information management standards and best practice – ISO 15489, ISO 17799, Code of Practice on the management of records under FOI, etc.
- data protection
- audit
- freedom of information.

Access

[*The organization*] will maintain an access control system which will ensure that any restricted information is only accessible to those authorized to see it. The system will also ensure that the movement of information in and out of the organization is controlled in such a way that records can be seen by different categories of users and that individuals/groups have access to information that enables them to undertake their activities effectively.

Decisions taken to withhold information will be recorded as part of the records management system's documentation procedures.

Security

[*The organization*] will take all reasonable steps to ensure that its records and information, and the procedures for managing them, are secure. Once recorded and registered they will be safe from alteration, misinterpretation or loss. Security procedures adopted include:

- complying with records management best practice and with information security standards (e.g. ISO 17799 and internal procedures on password and user identification)

- ensuring that staff have the requisite skills and knowledge to meet the security requirements of the records and information management system, including the creation and registration of records and metadata without loss of context and control
- auditing systems and procedures to ensure compliance with security requirements
- managing a business continuity plan to ensure that records and information are always available when required, even in the event of a disaster or changes in technology
- ensuring that vital records and information are backed up and safe from technical failures.

Preservation

[*The organization*] will ensure that its records and information are preserved during any change in the infrastructure that manages them so that they are still able to meet the requirements of this policy. Such change will include:

- the technology that processes the records
- organizational structures
- definition of terms used in the management of records and metadata
- revisions to the file plan resulting from changes in functions.

Policy review

[*The organization*] will follow this policy within all relevant procedures and guidance used for operational activities. Interpretation of the policy will be monitored and there will be regular planned inspections by Quality Services staff and Internal Auditors to assess how the policy is being put into practice. These inspections will seek to:

- identify areas of good practice which can be used throughout [*the organization*]
- highlight where non-conformance to the procedures is occurring
- if appropriate, recommend a tightening of controls and make recommendations as to how compliance can be achieved.

5

Information survey

This chapter examines a prerequisite for implementing new records and information management systems – the information survey.

One of the key undertakings in the planning and implementation of new records management systems is the information survey. You may know it also by the name of 'records audit' or 'information audit'. It is one of the most important processes that a records manager will undertake.

In general, an information survey provides an objective assessment of an organization's record- and information-keeping practices and procedures. It is the first and most important step in gaining control of records and information, providing a basis for both physical and intellectual management decisions. It is also a useful tool in assessing the level of knowledge of records management in an organization. Where information asset registers have been compiled, organizations may find these a useful source document for populating the information survey and they may even lead to significant savings in the survey process.

The objective of a survey is to produce a comprehensive list of all the records that your organization holds – paper, electronic, microform, etc. In the context of electronic records management the survey should not result merely in a list of application systems. It needs to gather information about each collection of records; in some cases, for example, the collection may be equivalent to an individual computer system, such as a database. In this context the term *record collection* is taken to mean a grouping of records with similar characteristics that can be managed together as a whole group; this would include making decisions for the group as a whole on filing, indexing, appraisal, migration and preservation. There are likely to be great variations between organizations but the important thing is to apply the term consistently within your own organization.

For less structured records the same office applications will produce records grouped in many different business areas. This may include electronic records in an unorganized or unmanaged environment, such as documents in general purpose folders on a network drive that have no discernible method of arrangement or, more likely, documents on a local hard drive of an individual or workgroup where the arrangement is not meaningful to others and does not relate to the corporate-wide scheme.

The survey should systematically list elements about each collection, such as:

- what records are held and the activities to which they relate (including electronic records which may be normally printed to paper and held in a paper record-keeping system)
- the groups/people who use and manage the records
- location of records
- records documentation (file lists, indexes, disposal schedules, etc.)
- volume of records
- date range of records
- frequency of use of the records and access requirements
- tracking systems for the records
- current records management system (including hardware and software)
- competence levels of records management staff.

In addition the survey should include the following elements that will help in the development of general records management principles and procedures and, more particularly, in the changes required to implement new electronic systems:

- a full understanding of the organization – the nature of its activities, its mission, objectives, components and operations
- level of staff awareness of records management
- what is regarded as the corporate record – paper or electronic or an integration of both
- portfolio of existing electronic systems, together with business cases and project documents (these will identify the business functions and activities to which each system relates and will avoid duplicating work already undertaken)
- work being undertaken by ICT departments in the development of electronic systems and infrastructure.

The survey provides a platform for further development of the records and information management system – principally a basis for developing the file plan, an authoritative document of what information is held so that requests for information (such as for business reasons or as the result of freedom of information enquiries) can be met and providing the necessary information to draw up disposal policies and schedules, which will ensure that records and information are kept only for as long as required.

Methodology
Planning

Many of the difficulties associated with introducing new records management procedures can be overcome by careful planning of the information survey. This planning should include:

- corporate support (in particular, commitment from top management)
- organization of the survey
- aims and objectives
- communication
- data collection
- compilation of forms.

Corporate support

The first step is to obtain senior management commitment. This should take the form of a directive from the Chief Executive/head of the organization, making reference to:

- the value and importance of managing records as an aspect of corporate policy
- an explanation of the role of the survey for the organization
- how long the survey will take
- the scope of the survey.

Organization of the survey

The choice of who will carry out the survey will depend very much on the nature and size of the organization. For example, in a small organization it would be possible for it to be undertaken solely by the records manager. In most cases, however, it will be more effective if a small team, representative of the organization as a whole, were to drive the survey forward. The records manager must maintain control of the survey and provide any advice and guidance required. Ask yourself also how far the internal auditors of the organization will want to be involved (if there is such a unit in the organization). There will often be an internal audit programme, sometimes on a rolling basis, and many organizational difficulties may be overcome by tapping into this.

There should be a survey timetable that clearly assigns responsibility for all activities, estimates the time for developing the survey in each area, and allows the necessary time to evaluate the survey results and to produce a report or plan.

Aims and objectives

Aims and objectives must be established before the survey is undertaken. These should parallel the aims of records management in general and may be short-term or long-term. Short-term aims are usually the basics of records management improvement programmes, such as the introduction of economical records storage and retrieval. In general the objectives of the survey will be one or more of the following, depending on circumstances and what is being aimed for:

- reappraising the records management structure of the organization
- creating a link between business functions and records creation
- determining the systems and equipment used for record keeping
- determining storage needs for active and semi-active records
- determining the use of records
- deciding how long records are required for business purposes
- determining the long-term (historical) value of records
- setting up legacy systems and hybrid records
- identifying obsolete records
- identifying vital records
- determining what information is held (for example, to meet freedom of information requirements or provide business information)
- providing the foundation for a reassessment of current records management policy, thus assuring the continuing improvement of records management practices.

The overall objective of the survey should therefore be to gather only the information that addresses the aims and objectives cited above. For example:

- identification of all the organization's records by series or collection and an understanding of their functional context and business needs will provide the basis for the disposal schedule
- categorization of the types of equipment will assist in systems improvement and in calculating savings.

Communication

There should be a communication strategy. People need to know not only that a survey is taking place but also why it is necessary. It needs to be put into context. Prior to carrying out the survey a notice should be sent to all managers and staff concerned, identifying the nature of the survey, its objectives, how it will affect their work, and when it will begin. It is often useful to hold orientation sessions with key staff, and to keep managers informed by the issue of progress reports. The communication plan needs to include a timetable of visits. Don't just turn up one morning, but at the same time don't give the client so much notice that they forget about it. Two weeks maximum is usual.

Consider what are the best ways to communicate this information:

- departmental meetings
- newsletters
- intranet
- informal discussions.

These vehicles might well include descriptions of the benefits that the organization will gain from the process.

Data collection

Before conducting the survey several items should be collected and studied:

- costs of office space, equipment, supplies and staff. Organizational unit costs are often calculated regularly for accommodation (including maintenance and running costs) and for staff (including support services)
- maps and plans of buildings, showing furniture and equipment
- copies of contracts with commercial storage companies, microfilming bureaux, computer services, etc.
- inventory of equipment, including computers and photocopiers
- organization charts that will give an understanding of the flow of information
- procedural manuals and forms
- copies of file lists or databases
- copies of previous studies.

Compilation of forms

If the survey requires that participants complete a form (as may often be the case), this form must only ask for information that is relevant to the aims and objectives of the audit. In this respect, therefore, there is no one standard form that is recommended.

Examples of two forms that have been used in the recent past in the UK are shown at the end of this chapter – one covering a broad survey aspect (used by a local authority but easily adaptable by any organization) and the other focusing particularly on electronic records.

Information collection

The collection phase of the survey needs careful consideration. You should only be collecting information that accords with the aims and objectives of the survey. It is a waste of time and resources seeking out information that you are not going to use.

All records within the scope of the survey must be included, not forgetting:

- confidential material (for example, personal files)
- private collections of official material (such as individual computer drives)
- all formats.

Collecting information during the survey is a time-consuming and labour-intensive exercise. There is no easy or quick way. There are three main methods:

1 *Physical observation*: a physical survey requires records staff to visit business areas and look into each item of records storage equipment or examine each computer drive, ask questions and complete a standard survey form. It is usually sufficient to sample a series or collection of records rather than examine individual records.

   The physical survey needs to be planned carefully and executed with a minimum of disruption. An initial investigation to establish the whereabouts, ownership, volume and condition of the records may be required to make the plan more effective. When the plan and timetable have been drawn up the detailed survey can take place.

   Four main actions form the key to finding out information from the survey:

   - *Find* every storage place (including tops of cabinets, disks, commercial storage, under desks)
   - *Look* at all the records and information in the location
   - *Ask* questions until understanding is complete
   - *Record* the information acquired for future analysis.

   Don't believe everything you are told! Seek evidence for the information given to you.
2 *Questionnaire*: it has been said that the reliability of data, which might be required to develop or support a hypothesis or serve as a prerequisite for introducing new procedures, is closely related to the size of the survey through which the data is obtained. Physical surveys can be programmed to cover all parts of an organization. The use of questionnaires or forms referred to above, however, relies on individuals to complete them accurately and in good time. Much time can be wasted chasing up missing forms and following up unclear information on completed, or partly completed, forms. Because of the heterogeneous nature of information resources, careful consideration should be given before deciding whether the use of a questionnaire or form will provide results comprehensive enough to enable crucial decisions to be made. Although a well constructed questionnaire or form that produces a high percentage response can be a sound, cost-effective approach to gathering information, greater coverage may be achieved through physical observation.

In addition, where questions are used, they must be framed so that they elicit relevant and accurate information. Open questions will encourage opinions and give freedom to respondents, but the analysis of free-ranging responses can be difficult. Closed questions lessen the chance of obtaining information which might be useful but which may not have been thought of. A balance of closed and open questions is ideal.

Open questions should direct the respondent to as specific an area as possible. For example, the following questions will produce different responses:

A. 'Having recently attended a records management course, what are your thoughts?'
B. 'You recently attended a records management course. What new skills do you think you acquired?'

Closed questions can be asked in a variety of ways:

- seeking a yes or no answer
- providing statement or answer boxes for ticks
- ranking scales, for levels of agreement to statements or order of priority of certain issues.

Whatever method or type of questioning is used, only one answer should be sought to one question. For example, the following is actually asking two questions:

> 'There have been too many leaks of confidential papers and managers should be doing more to prevent leaks occurring.'
> Agree...........|...........|...........|...........|...........|...........Disagree

Consideration should be given to the issue of anonymity. If names are not included on completed questionnaires it may cause difficulties in checking the extent of replies received. However, replies might be more honest and open if the respondent is not required to include their name on the form.

3 *Interviewing*: formal or informal interviews can be held with key members of staff to elicit the information required by the survey and this information entered on a suitable form. These might be carried out in one-to-one situations or with small groups of staff from discrete areas of the organization's business. Whatever method is adopted, it is vital to target the person or persons who have most knowledge about the records in the framework in which the survey is set. For example, it is not always the head of a unit or department; it may be a clerk or data processor who has been in charge of record keeping for several years.

Recommended approach: probably the best method is a combination of all these methods:

— send the questionnaire or form to key personnel in each business area

— ask them to complete the questionnaire or form as far as possible and retain it

— make an appointment (for up to one hour) at which the issues raised by the questionnaire or form can be discussed and clarified

— use the appointment as an opportunity to look at some records and storage equipment.

Surveyor

Who undertakes the survey will depend on the size of the exercise. Ideally it should be the records manager but it may be too much for one person. If there are staff in the records management unit, it may be a good training/development opportunity for them to participate in the survey under the guidance of the records manager. You may want to employ the services of a consultant and there are many who are available and willing to undertake such work.

Evaluation of results

The task of analysis and evaluation of the data from the survey should be carried out promptly as delay can make the findings obsolete. Evaluation should be made with a use for the information in mind. Records management is meant to improve records and information systems for the people who use them. A survey that results in only a statistical report is of no use. Information gathered from the survey will enable consideration to be given to several issues, for example:

* records which are valueless and could be destroyed immediately – identified from the survey form by low or nil usage rate, or duplication
* inactive records which could be removed to storage – closed files no longer required for reference which can be removed to cheaper accommodation
* computers being used inefficiently – the evaluation should take the opportunity to assess whether existing systems for managing electronic records, indexes or databases are being put to good use and are improving efficiency
* records or information which could be consolidated, including the elimination or reduction of duplication – evidence of duplication should be highlighted so that resources are used most efficiently
* protection of the records against loss, damage, etc. – the system or type of equipment used should take into account the value of the records, including those which may be of archival value
* effectiveness of systems (filing, indexing, etc.) – staff and user comments may point the way to the need for improvement.

Only when issues such as these have been considered can plans for improvement, appraisal or new programmes begin.

Reporting

Quantitative data from the survey can be presented in tabular form (e.g. number of different types of storage equipment), with charts (e.g. percentage of records covered by disposal schedules) or by graphs (e.g. comparison of number of staff and amount of records serviced).

Qualitative data, such as physical condition or staff comments, will need to be presented in narrative form.

The survey report should frame recommendations that are clear and which are constructive proposals for improvement or development. They should be short and supported by facts in the report. They may be one of several types:

1 *educational* – where the recommendation is long term or developmental, a timetable should be considered.
2 *influential* – where contact or negotiation and persuasion are needed, consideration should be given to who the important figures might be, whether they have been involved, and who might be able to contribute to implementation of the recommendation.
3 *threatening* – where some areas might be threatened by a recommendation, the balancing advantages must be taken into account.
4 *enforcing* – tightening up of procedures may lead to significant changes in culture or attitude.
5 *redeploying* – where existing procedures or systems may have to change, there may also be implications in budgets, timetable, training, etc.
6 *cost saving* – where costs can be measured with reasonable certainty, the report should set out the cost benefits clearly.

The survey report should be as short as possible. There should be a summary that concentrates on major findings and recommendations, a brief narrative to illustrate evidence gathered during the survey, and factual data.

Recommended structure of the report:

- *executive summary* (this is often the only part of a report which many people will read, so it needs to highlight major issues and recommendations in a clear and concise way)
- *introduction and background* (why the survey was commissioned, respective roles of the client and surveyor in the process)
- *methodology*
- *findings* (general and specific to business areas; data should be in annexes, e.g. people seen, file list, inventory, breakdown of storage equipment, etc.)
- *recommendations*
- *summary of recommendations* (number and short/concise, referring to paragraphs in the main body of the report).

Next steps

If the information survey has been undertaken in advance of the development of a business case for electronic records management (see the discussion under Principle 3 in Chapter 1), the next logical step is to develop that case. If the business case for the electronic records management project has been agreed, it is not likely that the report will sit on a shelf/desk indefinitely. It will form the basis for taking the project forward, first of all enabling the file plan to be developed.

Consider giving presentations on the outcomes of the survey – to management boards, departmental meetings and similar gatherings. Use established channels of communication to promote the report's recommendations – the intranet, newsletters, etc.

Records managers and others involved in information surveys need to be patient and flexible. It can be frustrating when much work has gone into the survey and there is a slow response to the recommendations. This is often the result of budget restraints but can also be because the rationale behind some aspects of the survey has been lost. Even though some of the data gathered during the survey may not be used immediately to improve record-keeping practices, it will be a valuable source of information for future developments.

One outcome of the information survey will be the identification of the extent to which existing records and information management systems satisfy your organization's need or requirements for information. In the context of this book we would expect precisely that in respect of the functions that the systems perform. If we are fairly certain that we will wish to go down the path of electronic records management, then it seems that we are already pretty convinced that existing systems are falling short in some areas. The information survey is designed to identify those areas so that they can be addressed effectively in the electronic records management project. However, the survey may also identify gaps in the records that are created – are sufficient records being created to enable the organization to discharge its functions effectively and provide sufficient evidence of its undertakings? Such an outcome will mean that a gap analysis will have to be undertaken to identify such records and information. While this is slightly beyond the scope of this book, there are several guidelines available on conducting such an analysis. Entering the term in your favourite internet search engine will bring them forward.

APPENDIX
Sample questionnaire/form 1

(Reproduced with kind permission from The National Archives)

Survey Questionnaire (*XXX District Council*)
Questionnaire on the Management of Records and Information

I should be most grateful if you could take some time out to complete the attached questionnaire prior to our meeting on xxxxxxxxxx. It should help to save time at the meeting and give us a good pointer to the type of information held and how it is used and disposed of.

If you would like to include any extra information or need to use an extra sheet, please attach the papers to the form. You need not return the form – it is being used to guide you in the direction of the records issues that will be raised.

Glossary of terms used

Section	a section/unit within a division working on a specific area of work (e.g. sustainability team in environmental health; countryside services in leisure). Where the division has a single function the term section should be interpreted as the division.
Disposal	the review and subsequent retention or destruction of records
Information	covering records in all formats (paper, electronic, etc.)
Registered file	official file forming part of a discrete series, classified and referenced in accordance with accepted practice (e.g. DAN/1/4/6)
Review	examination of a record to see if it has any further administrative or historical use
Unregistered file	informal folders or information held by individuals, neither of which are on a standard system
Vital records	those records without which a section could not continue to operate, and which contain information needed to re-establish the section in the event of a disaster

Thank you for your co-operation

1. Date completed:	2. Branch and function:

3. Person completing form and contact details:

4. What main categories of information does your section hold? (e.g. planning applications, registers of electors, policy files)

5. How information is held in your section. Please tick formats below (take all categories as one source of information): – registered files – personal network drive (h) – unregistered – personal disk drive (c) – floppy disk – other – network drive (f)	6. How much of this information is held on more than one of the formats (%)?

7. Does your section have a policy for disposal of your records, including electronic? If so, please give outline details (continue on a separate sheet)

8. What do you consider to be your vital records?	9. What indexes/finding aids does the section hold to help you locate records? (e.g. manual list, database) Do you use standard terms/naming conventions?

10. How much of the information held by your section is not used for current work (%) (including off-site storage)?

11. Where and how does your section store records (e.g. 4-drawer cabinets, open shelves, etc.)? Please indicate how many items of each type of equipment.

12. What and how much (%) information is currently made available to:

the general public?

shared with other branches in XXDC?

other authorities/organizations?

13. Please indicate what and how much other information in your section, if any, could be made available to:

the general public?

shared with other branches in XXDC?

other authorities/organizations?

14. What requests do you receive for the information that your section holds (please tick)?

Public representatives (MPs etc.)   Internal

Companies/organizations   Public

15. How much time do you spend looking for information each week (please tick)?

Less than 1 hr   1–3 hrs   4–6 hrs   7–10 hrs   Over 10 hrs

16. How often do you NOT find what you want (please tick)?

Never   Rarely   Sometimes   Often   Constantly

Sample questionnaire/form 2

Inventory of Record Collections Survey Form

Record collection and reference		
Description		
Originator		
Subject terms		

Open date	Closed date	Cut-off date

Physical formats		

Owner	Physical location	

Access constraints		Protective markings

Links to paper files		
Source		
Business function		
Disposal period		
Disposal action		

Signed .... Date ....

Description of information

Record collection and reference   Title by which the record collection is commonly identified, such as folder name, collection name or database name. Include the collection's reference number(s) where it exists.

Description   Brief description of the record collection, showing its role and purpose and any other important physical or intellectual characteristic. It may also include background and uses to which the information in the record collection is put.

Originator   The work group, section or other users who create the records in the course of their work. This may or may not be the same group which uses the records for business purposes.

Subject terms   Relevant subject terms from a controlled vocabulary or thesaurus (if used) or uncontrolled keywords that have been allocated to the collection (if any). This should be terms that would be used when seeking this information resource. The terms will be used when developing the file plan and for assisting in retrieval.

Open date   The date on which the record collection was opened or the creation date of the earliest document it contains.

Closed date   The date on which the record collection was deemed closed (if any) or the date of the last document it contains.

Cut-off date   The regular date used to separate parts of a continuing record collection for management purposes (for example, the end of the financial year, quarterly, monthly).

Physical formats   Application types (hardware and software) in which records are created and held in this collection, either directly by an end-user or by extraction from a larger set of electronic information. This information will enable the system to be audited and will support long-term preservation (including migration).

Owner   The workgroup, section or other users who manage or control the record collection. The custodian or responsible person for ensuring quality, coverage, accuracy, etc. The person or body who controls access or distribution.

Physical location   The current physical location of the record collection – the computer system on which it is held, the data archive store, the network location, etc.

Access constraints   Any restriction on use of the record collection or access constraints on particular user groups.

Protective markings   Security markings given to the record collection or parts of it (e.g. restricted, confidential).

Links to paper files   Reference or other identifying link to parts of the record collection that are held in paper form.

Source   Identification of any other record collection from which records in this collection are copied or moved.

Business function   The business function which requires the records in the collection for its own business purposes. This function will determine the length of time the records need to be kept for accountability, legal, operational or any other reason.

Disposal period   Scheduling information on the periods or events that determine
    retention of records in the collection.
Disposal action   Scheduling information on the characteristics and conditions of
    disposal for the collection, which may be destruction or transfer to an archive.

6

File plan

This chapter describes the most crucial aspect of the design of the electronic records management system – the file plan. It examines the key elements that make up the process – functional design, naming conventions and the management of e-mail within the plan. At the end of the chapter is a sample list of requirements for file plans and an example of a file plan. It is worth quoting the oft-repeated extract from guidance issued by The National Archives:

> **The departmental business classification scheme (file plan) should be recognized as the principal intellectual instrument in records management activities and should be devised and implemented to support the management of the creation and disposal of records and, where possible, the management of security of and access to the records.**
> **(Business Classification Scheme Design (The National Archives, 2003))**

Introduction

Already we have run up against one confusing aspect of this part of electronic records management – that of terminology. The term 'business classification scheme (BCS)' has been used widely to mean the file plan. In reality, BCS is a product of business analysis. It is used in management techniques and processes that involve organizational and business change. Such schemes (and there have been several types) are extremely useful and closely related to file plan structure but they are not the same thing. The file plan is something more than a classification scheme. It is a structure that is a reflection of records management principles – in particular taking into consideration appraisal, disposal, access and the management of specific types of record (such as case files). The overall purpose of creating, using and managing records is to *support* the business of an organization. For these reasons this book will use the term 'file plan'.

New considerations on file plans have arisen over the last few years largely as a result of the increasing use of electronic records management systems. This is not to say that the new approaches are not equally applicable to paper systems. Indeed, it has often been said, with some justification, that paper record-keeping systems and electronic records management systems should mirror each other. The purpose of the file plan, however, is to achieve intellectual control over both by ensuring that all the records and information of your organization are maintained consistently. It is clearly not conducive to good business practice to have two different systems operating together.

It almost goes without saying that inadequate or failing classification schemes for paper systems should not be transferred or replicated for the implementation of ERM. Moving to the electronic environment provides an opportunity to make improvements and develop a tool to meet business needs.

A corporate filing system should form the basis of your organization's information resource. A standardized file classification system has the following advantages:

- it ensures a clear record exists of how various series of records were created, by whom they were created, when they were created and for what purpose – this is important in meeting the demands of business efficiency and transparency, and also in providing contextual information for future researchers
- it provides systematic and economical storage of records
- it provides timely retrieval of records
- it provides ready identification of records for review and disposal
- it prevents the duplication of information.

See Table 6.3 (page 102) for a sample list of requirements.

Aims and objectives

The main purposes of a file plan may be summarized as:

- providing links between records that originate from the same activity or from related activities
- determining where a record should be placed in a larger aggregation of records
- assisting users in retrieving records
- assisting users in interpreting records
- assigning and controlling retention periods
- assigning and controlling access rights and security markings.

Three important considerations should underpin the design of the file plan:

1 *Simplicity* – the file plan must reflect functions, activities and tasks that are easily recognizable by users (this usually means that it must align itself with business processes as set out in corporate documents such as visions, policy statements,

business plans, aims and objectives). The bottom line is that in (as far as possible) every case it must be obvious into which file or folder a document should be placed.

2 *Consistency* – the file plan must have rules and guidelines that ensure all staff/users follow the same procedures. Inconsistencies typically manifest themselves as duplicate files/folders, documents on the same activity being separated, and misnaming of documents.

3 *Flexibility* – the file plan must be adaptable. It must be designed so that new files and folders can be fitted in as and when required, while still adhering to the principles of structure.

In designing a file plan it is vital to give full consideration to the views of users. The user's experience and perhaps even their acceptance of the electronic records management system may be affected by such considerations as:

- the number of levels in use in the file plan (in general more than four or five levels can be confusing even where they are collapsible, although in a very large organization this may be difficult to avoid)
- the browsing interface of the ERM system (particularly whether it enables the view of all the levels of the file plan and/or whether the folders as well as the file plan can be viewed in the same window)
- a large number of levels can be mitigated to a degree by users having 'stored favourites', saved searches and other tools at their disposal but these also militate against the free sharing of information that is often one of the drivers for ERM
- the approach taken by the implementation to the issue of whether folders containing records are permitted at and above the lowest level of the classification scheme, as opposed to just below it
- the other retrieval support tools available either as a part of the ERM system package itself or elsewhere in the technical environment.

Approach to producing a file plan

User consultation

User consultation is important for successful implementation of the file plan. Support will be needed to help users adapt to viewing, browsing and retrieving information in a variety of new ways.

User interface issues

The user interface needs to present a comprehensible and 'friendly' aspect to the end user. A purist functional approach is unlikely to be successful if the semantics of the file plan – however robust and consistent in theory – is not understandable to them. Substantial consultation should be conducted with user groups on whatever solution is proposed by the ERM project to ensure that there is sufficient acceptance and 'buy-in' by end users. Training on the file plan during implementation will also be required to ensure that they know how to use it and understand that it has been designed for purposes other than the management of current information, – for example, disposal management.

General issues with introducing a corporate file plan

It is an important consideration how users are to adapt to being able to view, browse and retrieve information in a variety of new ways in the electronic environment. As we have seen in the business case, this is an important part of the realization of benefits from the introduction of electronic records management.

In the paper environment, as the main view of the 'corporate' holding was only normally available to registry staff, users tended to interact with those staff as intermediaries and a limited subset of the organization's records closely related to the business unit in which they were employed. Records were generally under the physical control of the business unit that created them until such time as activity access had declined to such a low rate as to allow their transfer to off-site storage facilities. Once there, until disposal, if they were viewed at all, it was most likely that any retrieval would be by the same organizational units. Secondary purposes of records emerged haphazardly in some instances but were hardly facilitated by information management practices. In the electronic environment, the full file plan will be made available to all users. Staff can independently identify existing records that may inform their work. Those records may have been created by a different business unit and not accessed for some time, but will be available to meet a current information need.

An important objective of the file plan is to make it corporate. A major rationale behind electronic records management – and one of its major benefits – is to make your entire organization's records and information available to everyone in the organization as and when they require it. This corporate approach also ensures that all staff are using up-to-date versions of documents, that they have a complete picture of the task or activity in which they are engaged and that there is no duplication of information or duplication of effort in finding it.

Intellectual structures

Commonly, the intellectual structures for a file plan fall into four types:

Functional

Functions → Activities → Transactions

- The functions that an organization carries out change less frequently than its organizational structure.

- As changes move functions between organizations, it is easier to restructure corporate filing systems.
- A strict functional approach will not support case files well.
- Records managers like functional structures (management is easier); users do not understand them and dislike them (hard to use).

Subject/thematic

- Enables a more common approach across information systems: EDRM, websites, intranets, etc.
- More easily recognized and understood by users, but …
- Interpretation and understanding may vary considerably between user groups.

Organizational

- Familiar structure to end users, perhaps from the paper environment, but high maintenance and subject to frequent change.
- Continuity over time is difficult.

Hybrid

- Enables compromise between a strict purist approach and operational flexibility.
- For example: functional at a broad level (with disposal rules mostly operating at that level), with subject-based sub-classes.

The functional approach

An organization's administrative arrangements often change – for example when priorities change or opportunities for efficiency gains are identified. In these instances, functional responsibilities may be moved between departments. Alternatively existing departments may be merged or split. When functions move, current and recent records usually follow.

Although their allocation is prone to variation, the actual functions of an organization themselves tend to be quite stable and change little over time. Thus, a functional approach to the file plan can make the relevant records easier to identify and relocate during times of administrative change.

One potential huge benefit of the functional approach is the appraisal of the business function (as opposed to the records themselves that it produces, a costly process which involves examining individual files and records within them) and the application of disposal criteria at a higher level as a result of this activity. Second, any changes in organizational structure or the file plan itself need not affect the operation of disposal, as long as records are allocated to a particular function.

If you are contemplating the introduction of an electronic records management system, you are probably well aware of the functions that your organization discharges and how they are structured. However, you may want to spend some time analysing the functions as part of the preparations for the electronic file plan. While you have a classification scheme for your paper records, perhaps you feel that this is inadequate and needs some changes before considering whether it is suitable for use in the electronic environment. Functional analysis involves identifying the business functions of an organization and breaking them down into activities, tasks and perhaps sub-tasks as opposed to existing records or the organizational structure. Various methods may be used, singly or in combination, including hierarchical analysis (top-down) and process analysis (bottom-up). Much of the information which you gleaned from the information survey will be valuable in this context.

Design

The design of the functional file plan should be based on the simple framework of:

Function
|
Activity
|
Task

Function: The largest unit of business process/procedure in the organization; major responsibilities, managed by the organization to fulfil its goals; high-level aggregate of activities

Activity: The major pieces of work performed by the organization to accomplish each of its functions; several activities are often associated with each function

Task: The smallest unit of business activity; tasks, not subjects or record types.

These definitions depend largely on the way the organization is structured and, to a certain extent, its traditions and culture. It is not easy to get everyone to agree on these levels and indeed, in some cases, on the definitions themselves. Another way of looking at it might be to regard functions as those high-level corporate undertakings that often feature in corporate plans and objectives. Apart from generic functions – such as HR, finance, buildings/estates/ accommodation, health and safety, press and public relations/marketing, records management, and freedom of information – they are those for which the organization was established. For example:

Department of Health

Primary Care Trusts

— Engaging with local populations to improve health and well-being
- improving health status
- contributing to well being
- protecting health

— Commissioning a comprehensive and equitable range of high-quality, responsive and efficient services
- assessing needs, reviewing provision and deciding priorities
- designing services
- shaping the structure of supply
- managing demand
- performance-managing providers

— Directly providing high quality responsive and efficient services
- physiotherapy
- pharmacy

etc.

Aylesbury Vale District Council

— Community Services
- housing needs and advice
- environmental health
- licensing
- environment support
- recycling
- dog warden
- pest control

— Environment and Planning
- planning
- development control
- architecture
- quality surveying
- landscape
- historic buildings

etc.

Essex Police

— Services
- firearms applications
- reporting crime
- road collision information
- keyholders

— Crime

- child protection
- community safety
- investigation

etc.

Activities might also be seen as those pieces of work that are typically undertaken by teams, units and sections within the functional department, division or group. For example, the human resources (HR) function will have the following activities:

- recruitment
- training
- welfare
- discipline.

Tasks are typically undertaken by individuals or smaller teams and units. Using the same HR example, the recruitment activity may comprise the following tasks:

- advertising
- interviewing
- examinations and tests.

The focus throughout compilation of the plan should be on functions and activities. Generic terms such as 'Committees', 'Policy', 'Procedures' and 'Minutes' must be avoided, particularly at the top two levels. The view is that, if someone is looking for committee minutes or papers, the search relates to a committee on a specific function or subject.

The functional approach will mean that there are likely to be high levels of the file plan which contain no records. There is no harm in this. These levels are part of the structure of the file plan and are essential in that they describe the corporate functions and meet the objectives of corporate appraisal and disposal. Taking the human resources structure above as an example, we have:

1 Human Resources
    - Recruitment
       — advertising
       — interviewing
       — examinations and tests.

There are almost certainly not going to be any documents at the top (functional) level (Human Resources). Individual documents will be more closely described than simply 'human resources' and will be filed in folders at the lower levels. There may not even be any documents at the second (activity) level (Recruitment), although it might (in this example) contain high-level policy documents on recruitment. Most of the documents in this area of the file plan are likely to be in folders at the third (task) levels.

The design approach describes three levels. It is possible that one or two more level(s) may be required, although these should be kept to a minimum to avoid complex and confusing structures (where, for example, it becomes uncertain in which folder to place a document). Procedurally the Records Manager must control the top two levels of the plan; staff themselves should be in a position to allocate folders at subsequent levels, but the records managers should be able to satisfy themselves that accepted file plan procedures are being properly followed.

The structure of the file plan might be represented graphically in Table 6.1 as follows:

Table 6.1 The structure of a file plan

Type	Levels		Description	Creator
Function	1	1	Classification	Records Manager
Activity	2	2		
Task	3	3	Record	User
Sub-task	4	4		
Sub-sub-task	5	5		

Folders which are created for classification/structural purposes only are in the shaded areas. The rest comprise folders in which records are stored.

Naming conventions and thesauri

The plan should incorporate a system of naming conventions so that records are described in a consistent manner over time. This will promote the efficient retrieval and disposal scheduling of records. The organization should be able to issue lists of accepted terms for particular descriptions or wording, and may even wish to go as far as compiling a thesaurus. In this context much work has recently been completed in the UK on the development of an Integrated Public Sector Vocabulary (IPSV) – an encoding scheme for populating subject metadata to index and categorize information across the public sector. This controlled vocabulary contains approximately 3000 preferred and 4000 non-preferred terms. Using a device such as this can make it easier for people to find the information resources they want on networks and systems such as the internet or internal documentation systems. For example, using a keyword such as 'jobs' typically fails to retrieve items described as 'vacancies', recruitment opportunities', 'situations vacant', etc. The IPSV needs to be used together with tools for applying the consistent names in metadata and search engines that read metadata. Detailed information on this can be obtained from the Cabinet Office website at: www.esd.org.uk/standards/ipsv/.

If individual units or sections of the organization have folders with the same or similar titles in the file plan can the staff of those units/sections be sure that they have the complete story in 'their' folders so that they are able to discharge their duties effectively? Indeed this highlights the corporate approach to the file plan – folders, records and documents do not belong to any individual, unit, section or department within the organization. They are not 'my' records or 'our' records in 'our' part of the file plan; they are corporate records in the corporate file plan – available to everyone who needs them. For example, there need only be one part of the file plan relating to generic functions like health and safety. Having folders in the file plan that are described as follows:

Health and Safety
   HR Department
     Accommodation
     VDUs
     Stress

  and

Health and Safety
   Finance Department
     VDUs
     Stress
     Safety inspections

is not conducive to the corporate approach and will clearly promote the duplication of material and effort. It is much better to have one area of the file plan that is accessible to all parts of the organization. Thus:

Health and Safety
   Accommodation
     Safety inspections
     Stress
     VDUs

Individually named documents will identify, if necessary, units and sections within the organization. For example, there may be several documents in the folder *Health and Safety – Safety inspections* named as follows:

- Finance Department
- HR Department
- Press Office

- Security Control Room

This raises another point on the naming of documents. The individual documents above need not have 'Health and Safety' or 'Safety inspection' in the title, since that is where they will appear in the file plan. If you were to enter a search term 'safety inspection', you will be shown the contents of that folder and be able to pick out the particular document or report that you want. Even entering the term 'HR Department' will take you to the appropriate document. There may actually be several documents in the file plan with the title 'HR Department' but they will be lodged under different activities or tasks. One of the common core requirements for ERM systems is for search engines to show the path (often called 'parents') of any document requested. Thus, in our example in Table 6.2, if you were to request 'HR Department', you may have several documents described on the screen as follows:

Table 6.2 Sample retrieval result

Title	Parent folder 2 (Activity)	Parent folder 1 (Function)	Date of document
HR Department	2007	Chief Executive Annual Reports	31/1/07
HR Department	Budget	Financial Planning 2006/07	1/4/06
HR Department	Safety inspections	Health and Safety	15/11/06
HR Department	Performance measurement	Corporate Business Planning	1/1/07

Organizations have their own cultures and style when it comes to the subject of terminology or, in this case, the naming of records and documents. However, some of the more common rules in naming convention schemes are:

Elements not needed – The following information is normally not needed in a name:

- Author
- Dates
- Department
- Folder name
- Type of document.

Free text description – In many systems there is a facility to add a 'free text' description of the document or record in a *comments* field. A free text description should bring out terms and concepts not immediately apparent from the record's name, or where it is filed. Ideally a free text description should not repeat terms found in the name or file plan classification.

Practices to avoid in naming

- don't include electronic file format information – e-mail, word document, etc.
- don't use default names or computer-generated names, e.g. 'document1', 'new folder', or 'untitled'
- don't use meaningless terms
- don't use generic names like 'latest version'
- don't base names on individual use or ownership e.g. 'John's really useful record'
- never use the words 'miscellaneous' or 'general' (they encourage poor filing practice – ending up with an amorphous mass of documents which are difficult to search and retrieve)
- don't compress two or more words into one word, e.g. 'planform' or 'bpcycle'; always separate words with spaces
- don't accept the e-mail subject as a name.

Abbreviations – never use abbreviations. For example, 'mtg' for 'meeting', 'Mins' for 'minutes', 'Corr' for 'correspondence', 'Reorg' for 'reorganization'. Abbreviations are incomplete words, and deviation from the full word often means that the ERM system is unable to retrieve the requested data or document. Abbreviations can be used inconsistently. Some words can be abbreviated in a number of ways. Users are less likely to use creative licence when entering the word in full, than when they are using abbreviations.

Acronyms – these are commonly used as shorthand for organizations and departments. For example, BBC, M & S, HMT. Organizations change frequently and the meaning of acronyms, while clear today, may be lost irretrievably in a matter of years or even months. However, individual organizations become very familiar with acronyms within their own areas and an authorized short list of permissible acronyms is often adopted as part of the naming conventions. To ensure maximum accessibility, it may sometimes be necessary to include both the acronym and the full words in the title. For example, Department for Constitutional Affairs (DCA).

Check spelling – spelling in all folder, document and record names should be accurate. Some systems are intolerant of name variations.

An alternative to a scheme of naming conventions is to use a structured thesaurus. There are many general subject thesauri available (e.g. Library of Congress or APAIS) as well as subject-specific thesauri (e.g. *Zoological Record Thesaurus* by Biosis, *Archaeological Monuments* by English Heritage, *GEMET Environmental Thesaurus* by the EEA). There are also quite a few thesauri that have been developed by central governments internationally, either subject-specific (e.g. Australia's *Department of Health and Aged Care Thesaurus*) or for whole-of-government (e.g. *Government of Canada Subject Thesaurus*). An organization-specific thesaurus can require substantial investment in its development and maintenance.

Metadata

A great deal has been written and said about metadata – its definition, its management and its role in records management. It is often described as 'data about data'. It may be more helpful to describe it as 'descriptive and technical document-ation'. Surfing the internet will reveal numerous slightly different definitions. What is certain, however, is that the term is used differently in different communities. Some use it to refer to machine-understandable information, while others use it only for records that describe electronic resources. There are three main types of metadata:

1 *Descriptive metadata* describes a resource for purposes such as discovery and identification. It might include elements such as title, abstract, author and keywords.
2 *Structural metadata* indicates how compound objects are put together – for example, how pages are ordered to form chapters.
3 *Administrative metadata* provides information to help manage a resource, such as when and how it was created, file type and other technical information, and who can access it.

Many different metadata schemes have been developed over the years in a variety of user environments. Some of the most common ones are:

- Dublin Core
- Text Encoding Initiative (TEI)
- Metadata Encoding and Transmission Standard (METS)
- Metadata Object Description Schema (MODS)
- Encoded Archival Description (EAD)
- E-Government Metadata Standard (e-GMS).

For more information on this subject, see Chapter 4 and have a look at the GovTalk website: www.govtalk.gov.uk/schemasstandards/metadata.asp.

Case files

The management of case papers in a file plan raises particular issues. It is often more convenient to classify a whole collection of case material at one level, presenting (in effect) a subject classification. This is perfectly acceptable since it meets one of the prime objectives of the file plan – user friendliness. Indeed, this is how the activity or task is conducted and it would be nonsensical to insist in breaking casework down in order to fit the intellectual structure of the file plan.

A case will normally possess an identifier ('ID') that is perfectly adequate for most purposes and generated from outside the immediate environment of the ERM system. Such things have evolved to suit the business needs of organizations in the paper environment. For example:

- an ID from a case management application with varying degrees of integration with the electronic environment
- a citizen's personal name
- an organization's name or reference number from an authoritative source
- a case ID (or other) as a structured element in folder titling.

Thus this self-indexation can be relied upon for most business purposes and it is possible to have the case files existing within a 'shallow' area of the classification scheme (i.e. with fewer levels).

E-mail

Policy

An e-mail policy is an essential business document for any organization as more and more business is being conducted by e-mail these days. E-mail is increasingly becoming the primary business tool for both internal and external communication and as a result needs to be treated with the same level of attention and importance as that given to the management of more formal reports and correspondence. In short, almost all e-mail is now part of an organization's official record. In the context of the development of a file plan, an e-mail policy must state explicitly that appropriate business records need to be maintained for audit and accountability purposes and that it must be recognized that e-mail should be treated as a record of a business activity when used in such a way. Failure to capture and maintain e-mail records could lead to difficulties when providing evidence about how and why a business function was undertaken or when answering requests for information.

Management

E-mail messages will naturally remain in the e-mail system until they have been dealt with/answered. It is common for individual inboxes to contain substantial numbers of messages. This being the case, and since an e-mail message may not always be clearly identifiable without reading the message itself, it can be hard to locate specific information. The task would be made easier if mailboxes were organized like mini-file plans so that like information is contained in the same folder (see Table 6.4). This would also greatly facilitate subsequent saving of e-mails into the corporate file plan. The e-mail policy should state explicitly that individual members of staff are responsible for managing their inboxes in this way.

It is now common practice for organizations to use automatic deletion from mailboxes after a specified period (typically three months) in order to prevent them becoming cluttered and inaccessible. Unrestricted use of mailboxes can also slow down the system for the organization as a whole.

All members of the organization must be able to identify which e-mail messages should be captured as a record into the electronic records management system. In most cases it will be obvious which these are – discussions, information distributed to groups of people, agreement to proceed and other exchanges relating to the discharge of business. In addition many e-mails will have attachments and a decision needs to be made as to whether both the message and the attachment should be captured. In most circumstances the attachment should be captured as a record with the e-mail message since the message more often than not provides the context within which the attachment was used.

Deciding who should be responsible for capturing the e-mail message and/or attachment into the ERM system involves the following guidelines which are commonly adopted:

- internal e-mail messages – the sender of the e-mail or initiator of an e-mail dialogue that forms a string of messages
- e-mail messages sent externally – the sender
- e-mail messages received by one person from an external source – the recipient
- e-mail messages received by more than one person from an external source – the person responsible for the area of work relating to the message.

It is sometimes the case, of course, that e-mail strings are longer than the three months at which many organizations initiate automatic deletion. In principle there is no reason why related e-mails cannot be managed within the electronic records management system rather than the inbox. In practice, however, it is usually convenient in such situations to move e-mails to the ERM system at convenient or significant points during the process.

The title of an e-mail does not always reflect the reason for capturing the message as a corporate record or make it obvious that it relates to other records with which it is being filed. If this is the case it should be re-titled at the moment of capture (using accepted naming conventions). All instances of 'FW' and 'RE' should be removed.

Table 6.3 Sample table of requirements for record organization and file plans

Ref	Requirement	M/HD/D*	Comments
1.1	The system must be able to support a records file plan which is able to represent a hierarchy of at least four levels and which can be pre-built before being populated with records.	M	
1.2	The file plan must enable textual description and separate alpha numerical coding for each level in the hierarchy and allow searching and retrieval using both methods.	HD	
1.3	The system must permit different branches of the file plan to be extended to a different number of levels. The minimum number of levels should be three.	HD	
1.4	The system must support a distributed file plan across the organization (HQ, regional and local offices, and remote users).	M	
1.5	The file plan must be synchronized across the system so that only one version of it is visible on the system at any one time.	M	
1.6	It must be possible for users to create new record folders or to restrict this to specified people.	M	
1.7	It should be possible to assign additional keywords or metadata to the file plan to assist users in locating the right part of the plan for specific records linked to keywords.	D	
1.8	It must be possible for users to navigate the file plan using a graphical user interface supporting browsing and graphical navigation of the folders and file plan structure.	M	
1.9	The system must provide for no fewer than 100 separate record types to be defined so that different types of record can be configured to capture only relevant metadata for the type of record.	M	
1.10	The system should offer an unlimited number of metadata fields to be attached to record types and new folders which should be configurable to accept text and numbers, and which should be subject to mandatory or optional completion and validation before acceptance by the system.	HD	
1.11	The system should allow for the unlimited creation of virtual electronic folders to act as the equivalent of paper folders to aggregate and store related records. Each folder must be attached to the file plan when opened.	D	
1.12	It should be possible to relate record types in a hierarchical relationship so that logically contained physical records can be entered on the system and the logical relationship maintained.	HD	
1.13	The file plan structure must support the use of open and closed folders and electronic and non-electronic records.	M	

Table 6.3 *Continued*

Ref	Requirement	M/HD/D*	Comments
1.14	The system should be able to support multiple record entries across the file plan without duplicate instances of the record.	D	
1.15	The system must allow for folders, sub-folders and records to be re-allocated to another folder or sub-folder.	M	
1.16	The system should be able to support the use of a keyword thesaurus to assist in consistent naming and metadata, compliant with ISO 2788.	HD	
1.17	The system must allow for cross-referencing of folders, sub-folders and all records within them.	M	
1.18	The system must support folder, sub-folder and record level metadata.	M	
1.19	The system must support navigation based searching to include folders, sub-folders and records, and direct text based searching.	M	
1.20	The system should automatically allocate sequential references to folders, sub-folders and records.		
1.21	The system must allow for reporting on the file plan structure, usage and changes.	HD	
1.22	The system must allow documents to be declared as corporate records at any stage during their life cycle. After declaration the records must become 'read only'.	M	
1.23	When a record has been declared a corporate record the system must not permit editing by any user.	M	
1.24	The system must integrate with existing desktop office software (such as e-mail and MS Office) running on XP so that a document can be saved directly into the system.	HD	
1.25	The system must automatically capture metadata derived from the operating system.	M	
1.26	The system should automatically capture any additional metadata created in MS Office and contained in the properties of individual documents.	HD	
1.27	The system must allow user entry and subsequent editing of specified metadata by authorized administration users and prevent non-authorized changes.	M	
1.28	The system should capture and relate the folder, sub-folder or record in its original form in terms of presentation and content.	D	
1.29	The system should enable multiple email attachments and embedded messages to be saved as a single record.	HD	
1.30	The system must record date, time and user information relating to a declared record.	M	

*M – mandatory; HD – highly desirable; D – desirable

These requirements are provided as a sample only. Organizations will have their own specific requirements based on their business processes and procedures as well as their business culture (Table 6.4).

Table 6.4 Example of a file plan
(Reproduced with kind permission from Natural England)

Function	Activity	Task
Shared Services	Strategic Services	
	Operational Services	
Corporate Governance	Audit	External audit
		Internal audit
	Boards	Executive Board
		Non-Executive Board
	Chairman's Office	
	Chief Executive	
	Compliance	Data Protection
		Freedom of Information
		Human Rights
		Public Records
	Directors' Portfolios	
	Environmental management	
	Environmental Futures	
	Guidance	
	Local management/policy	Advice
		Advocacy
		Consultation
		Joint ventures
		Liaison
		Research
	Natural England vesting	
	Performance management	
	Policy management/development	
	Project management	
	Quality management	
	Regional management/policy	Advice
		Advocacy
		Consultation
		Joint ventures
		Liaison
		Research
		Region 1
		Region 2
		Region 3
		Region 4
		Region 5
		Region 6
		Region 7
		Region 8
		Region 9
	Risk management	
	Strategic planning	National Programme
		Organizational development
Human Resource Management	Agency staff	
	Attendance management	Flexi time
		Leave
		Overtime
		Sickness recording

Table 6.4 *Continued*

Function	Activity	Task
		Timekeeping
	Conditions of service	
	Discipline	
	Employee relations	
	Manpower planning and organization	
	Performance management	
	Pensions administration	
	Policy and strategy	
	Recruitment	Advertising
		External
		Internal
		Interviewing
		Job descriptions
		Transfers
		Vacancies
	Staff Files/Folders	Individually named case folders
	Training	Course administration
		Development programmes
		Executive Leadership Handbook
		Induction
		Staff Handbook
	Welfare	
	Work experience	
Financial Management	Accounting	Audit
		Consolidated Fund
		Contingency Fund
		Guidance
		Invoices
		Payments processing
		Receipts processing
		Refunds
		Reports
		Systems development
	Asset management	Additions
		Asset audit
		Asset register
		Capitalization
		Compliance
		Cost centres
		Current assets
		Current liabilities
		Depreciation
		Disposals
		Locations
	Budget management	Final budgets
		Fund raising
		Planning
		Public Expenditure Survey (PES)
		Reconciliation
		Reports
		Requests

Table 6.4 *Continued*

Function	Activity	Task
	Commercial support	
	Contracting	
	Credit management	
	Income Generation	
	Insurance	
	Investments	
	Pay	
	Pensions	
	Planning and Strategy	
	Procurement	
	Tax management	
ICT Management	Infrastructure	Disposal
		Fault reporting
		Licensing
		Help Desk
		Information security
		Network maintenance
		Server maintenance
		Spatial data management
		Storage
		Strategy
		Web development
Knowledge and Information Management	Access to information	
	Archives	
	Knowledge management	
	Records Management	Compliance
		Forms development
		Image capture
		Disposal scheduling
		Tracking
Estates and Facilities Management	Acquisition and Disposal	
	Buildings maintenance	Works programmes
		Building 1
		Building 2
	Catering	
	Cleaning	
	Copying	
	Environmental monitoring	
	Equipment	
	Grounds maintenance	
	Incidents	
	Lifts	
	Mechanical and Electrical Services	
	Outsourcing	
	Pest control	
	Planning and Development	
	Postal services	
	Reception facilities	
	Relocation	
	Security	Advice and guidance

Table 6.4 *Continued*

Function	Activity	Task
		Bomb control
		Equipment
		Inspections
		Reporting
		Reviews
	Transport	Car Hire
		Rail travel
Occupational Health	Health and Safety	Community safety
		Compliance
		Emergency planning
		Monitoring
		Risk management
Communication	Campaigns	
	Education	
	Events	
	Press and Public Relations	
	Publicity	Internal
		External
Stakeholders	UK	
	International	
Legal Services	Advice	
	Land registration	
	Litigation	
	Management of legal activities	
	Planning controls	
Designated Areas	National Parks	
	Areas of Outstanding Natural Beauty	
	National Nature Reserves	
	Sites of Special Scientific Interest	
Conservation		
Land Use		
Funding		
Research, Science, Evidence		

Appraisal methodology

This chapter examines how appraisal methodologies need to adapt to the evaluation of electronic records. It includes an examination of the role of disposal scheduling, the impact of legislation and destruction of electronic records. At the end of the chapter is a sample table of requirements for retention and disposal.

Before considering appraisal in an electronic environment, we need to be clear about some of the key terms used. Different words and phrases are used by different people in the profession but, for the purposes of this book, the following have been adopted:

- *Appraisal* – the process of evaluating an organization's activities to determine what records should be kept, and for how long, to meet the needs of the organization, the requirements of government or other accountability, and the expectations of researchers and other users of the records.
- *Disposal* – the implementation of appraisal and review decisions. These comprise the destruction of records and the transfer of custody of records (including the transfer of selected records to an archival institution). They may also include the movement of records from one system to another (for example, paper to electronic).
- *Disposal schedule* – a list of collection/series of records for which predetermined periods of retention have been agreed between the business manager and the records manager.
- *Retention* – the continued storage and maintenance of records for as long as they are required by the creating or holding organization until their disposal.
- *Review* – the examination of records to determine whether they should be destroyed, retained for a further period, transferred to an archival institution or presented to a third party.

The process of appraisal is important to ensure that the records that should be kept are kept for as long as they are needed – either for finite, identified periods or as archives – and that disposal decisions are properly justified and documented. Appraisal also includes determining what the records are; who creates them and why; how they relate to the creating organization's functions and to other records; and how, when and by whom they were used. All this information is required in order to be able to make a valid judgement on the length of time for which records should be kept. Analysis of the context of a record is a vital part of the overall process of appraisal.

Current appraisal methodologies in the UK public sector are derived from paper record-keeping systems. The tradition is that decisions about long-term value require the passage of time to be made successfully. In the electronic environment, however, this is no longer possible, even after a small passage of time. The significance of the record will be difficult to judge because of the loss of contextual information.

General approach

There are three key reasons why we cannot use traditional methods of appraisal for electronic records.

Time

When we store paper records we expect to be able to retrieve them and understand them after many years (providing certain basic environmental conditions are met). Not so with electronic records. If we store digital material over a period exceeding 5–7 years we may well find that the technology by which they were created has become obsolete and we can only partly understand the records or perhaps understand them fully only after the expenditure of a great deal of resources. The appraisal and disposal of electronic records, whether for business or historical purposes, cannot be delayed because

- information about the records (and the technological expertise) may be lost when they become inactive. Even after a small passage of time metadata may be lost, information about the creating organization may not be present and, because crucial records may be surrounded by millions of other records, their significance may be difficult to evaluate
- maintaining records which have no value is costly, especially when systems and technology change and they have to be migrated
- the records may be destroyed inadvertently.

The electronic records manager has to strike a balance between losing all the information as a result of not appraising the records in time and losing some of the information because it falls outside the appraisal principles (see 'application' below).

Context

The sheer volume of electronic records and their complexity make it difficult to adopt traditional methods of appraisal. The complexity arises largely from the situation that content and context are separated. An electronic record lacks the intellectual unity which provides help in judging its value. It consists of several components which are not all visible to the user:

- Data and information content
- Software
- Hardware
- Storage medium
- Metadata.

This lack of information for the appraiser means that different approaches have to be taken – an analysis of the context needs to be undertaken before any evaluation can be carried out.

Application

Far more records are created in an electronic environment than in the paper world. Our work patterns have changed over the years and we have an unquenchable thirst for more information. Electronic systems will often create this information automatically – it does not have to be entered in the form we want to use it. This mass of information cannot be appraised in the same way as paper records. A higher-level evaluation needs to take place. This may mean losing some information which might normally have been selected in paper methodologies or even selecting some information which would normally have been discarded with traditional methodologies. The electronic records manager needs to strike a balance between this possible loss and losing all the information by not appraising in time (see 'time' above).

Paper legacy

It is worth noting and recognizing at this point that records managers are still left with a huge paper legacy even though we are heading quickly towards the management, storage and retrieval of our information electronically. The legacy is there because paper appraisal methodologies have had the luxury of being able to make decisions about long-term value after the passage of time (typically 25 to 30 years). Even though new access regimes and legislation mean that information must be readily available almost as soon as it is created, the process of evaluating that information for long-term retention remains locked in this traditional methodology. In addition, not all parts of the public sector have been able to approach records appraisal in a structured manner, often because of the lack of resources or the lack of support from key areas of the organization. However, even in these areas, the paper legacy is there, but it is complicated by its lack of structure and co-ordination between stakeholders. A further complication lies in the existence of hybrid records – where new information is created electronically but is part of or linked to other information that exists in paper form. It makes sense that closely linked records should be appraised together even though this overrides established methodologies.

Macro appraisal

Methodology

For the reasons set out above we need to appraise electronic records by looking at records from a high-level perspective rather than from the perspective of each discrete record. This macro approach involves:

- examining the background to the organization – the legislation under which it operates and its administrative history
- analysing the organization's structure to establish what it did, how it did it and why it did it; also what it does now and how it does it
- identifying relationships with other organizations and with stakeholders.

The focus of this process is on identifying which parts of the organization contain information that is likely to be of long-term value. It should highlight those parts of the file plan that are likely to contain information worthy of retention. The results of the analysis should be documented so that they can be referred to in future appraisals. This document – let's call it the Appraisal Report – will be dynamic in that it should be monitored and revised or updated as and when required. The analysis will help in the development of disposal schedules and will serve as a useful guide to future development of file plans. A sample Appraisal Report is provided at the end of this chapter.

When folders in the file plan that contain information fitting the selection criteria are identified they will be selected and transferred accordingly.

What to retain – business requirements

Organizations should only retain those records that they need for the undertaking of current operations. When that need expires, the records should be disposed of. Only the business area itself can decide how long this retention period should be. However, experience shows that there is often a great reluctance to destroy records under this heading – thoughts of 'it might come in useful', '. . . just in case', 'what if we get an enquiry?', etc. often prevail. Just consider how often you refer to closed records. What really are the consequences if you have to turn down a request for information because the record has been destroyed? Essentially this is a risk assessment exercise – what risks will you be encountering if you destroy particular information?

Are those risks acceptable to the organization? Keeping records that you do not need wastes resources. It can be dangerous to think that you can keep everything in electronic form because storage is so cheap. Up to a point this is true, but what happens when systems are upgraded and you need to migrate information to new platforms or new software? Then you will find how expensive record keeping can become. A robust disposal policy is at the heart of good records management and good business management. You should always set aside time to destroy worthless information. It is an essential part of the design of electronic records management systems.

What to retain – legal requirements

Primary legislation (enacted by Parliament) and secondary legislation (regulations, instruments, etc. issued under Acts of Parliament) may establish policy that will determine or influence the period during which records must be retained.

In the UK the Limitation Act 1980 prescribes a time limit on the period within which a party can commence legal proceedings or (in some circumstances) require notice of a claim to be given to the other party in potential legal proceedings. This has an important effect on the retention of records, since organizations have to manage the risk of actions arising from contracts and duties of care to employees, citizens and others. The retention of records plays an important part in this. The period in the Limitation Act needs to be validated against other needs before being assumed to match the retention period of relevant records. The key limitation periods in the Act are as follows in Table 7.1.

Table 7.1 Limitation Act 1980 – key periods

Cause	Period	Comments
Negligence	Within 6 years of the negligent act or omission	
Latent damage	3 years from the date of knowledge	Negligent latent damage is barred by way of long stop after 15 years from the negligent act or omission
Contract	Within 6 years of the breach of contract	
Contract under seal (deeds)	Within 12 years of the breach of contract or deed	
Recovery of land	Within 12 years of the right accruing	After 12 years the title of the person is extinguished
Personal injury or death	3 years	
Recovery of goods	6 years	
Sums recoverable by statute	6 years	
Rent recovery	6 years	

Note: this does not constitute legal advice and, in all cases, organizations should check with their legal departments

You will need to ensure that appraisal procedures are consistent with the fair processing principles of the Data Protection Act 1998. The Act requires the disposal of personal data in a timely, orderly manner and forbids its retention without good reason. Such information is invariably an integral part of the record and will have to be managed as part of it, meaning that the disposal of the record will have to take account of the processing of the personal data.

There are a number of other statutory obligations on public bodies to retain, withhold or release records. Those that you are likely to encounter are summarized below. As with all legal matters of this nature, records managers should confirm their actions with formal legal advice.

1 *Companies Acts 1985 and 1989* – set out minimum retention periods for company accounts and for the records of dissolved companies.
2 *Employers' Liability (Compulsory Insurance) Act 1969* (and subsequent regulations) – sets out a minimum retention period for employers' liability insurance certificates.
3 *Financial Services Act 1986* (and related regulations) – minimum retention period for salary advices.
4 *Health and Safety at Work Act* (and associated regulations) – sets out minimum retention periods for several categories of records, including accident books, dangerous occurrences reports, control and use of hazardous substances (COSHH), risk assessment, monitoring of working environments and employees' health, and disposal of waste.
5 *Value Added Tax Act 1994* – sets out minimum retention periods for various financial documents.

What to retain – historical requirements

Every organization should have a policy on what records and information it will earmark for permanent preservation because of their historical value. It should be drawn up after consultation with appropriate stakeholders and should be published.

There is no doubt that, over the past twenty years or so, research into archives has diversified. Records of national, local and other archives establishments have attracted attention from a broader range of disciplines. Historians themselves now choose to study a much wider range of subjects. In numerical terms the most striking change has been the increase in researchers studying the history of their families or their localities. In common with an increasing number of other users of records and archives, genealogists are not necessarily interested in what the records show us about the government's own policies and processes. Their focus is more on the individuals and communities with which the government had dealings. It is important, therefore, that any acquisition or collection policy should keep pace with current research trends and draw upon a value system that is relevant to contemporary studies and research. Consequently, such a policy should be flexible and fluid.

The kinds of questions that should be asked when considering the selection of historical records are:

1 *Is the information unique?* The appraisal of particular records should not be an isolated undertaking. Decisions need to be taken in context with other records. Information in the records may be wholly or substantially available in a variety of other sources, such as other media, other parts of the organization (for example, regional or local offices) or published works.

2 *Are the records related to other records selected for permanent preservation?* Records that add significantly to the value of other historical records may warrant selection.

3 *How significant are the records for recording the history of the organization?* If preservation of the organization's administrative history (its 'memory') is a priority, they may be worth selection.

4 *How significant are the records for research purposes?* In many areas of the public sector there is more emphasis on the selection of records for research. This is the most difficult evaluation to make. Something that may not be of great research value now may be of significant value in the future. Regardless of the difficulty, it is important to consider this question in making appraisal decisions. We should take into account the nature and extent of current research and, by regular contact with record users, try to make inferences about the anticipated use of selected records.

5 *How usable are the records?* With electronic records there may be considerable technological issues that affect the usability of the records. Extraordinary measures may need to be taken to make the information accessible. Close co-operation with ICT staff will determine this and the decision may be that the resource input is too great to warrant selection.

Disposal scheduling

The need to appraise electronic records earlier than has traditionally been the case with paper records is not difficult to achieve. The greater use of disposal schedules will facilitate the process, and you will recall from the description of the information survey in Chapter 5 that disposal schedules are a natural by-product of that exercise. In effect, appraisal and disposal decisions may now often be made before the records to which they relate even exist. Disposal decisions will be one of the metadata elements associated with each record at the point of capture within an electronic records management system and storage in the file plan.

Disposal schedules are the most important element of any records management system and, if possible, they take on added importance in an electronic environment. For example, an electronic records management system has the potential to administer disposal more globally, bringing an unprecedented degree of transparency and auditability to the process. Just as in the paper environment, the schedules cover series or collections of records for which a retention period can be determined for the whole series/collection and agreed between an organization's business manager (for the area in which the records were created or are held) and the records manager. The schedules identify and describe each record collection or series, not the individual records they contain. If possible, all the records of an organization should be covered by disposal schedules. In general they have far-reaching benefits:

- faster retrieval of important records from systems due to the early elimination of records of no further value
- clear instructions on what happens to records when they are no longer needed to support the organization's business (so that everyone knows what to do with them)
- definitive periods of time for which records should be kept and remain accessible (enabling better management of file plans)
- consistency in retention of records across the organization
- compliance with legal and regulatory requirements
- evidence of what records were created but destroyed (for example, for freedom of information compliance)
- highlighting of records which require special handling due to sensitivity
- identification of historically important records at an early stage
- elimination of duplicate records at the earliest possible opportunity.

A disposal schedule should contain the following elements:

- the name of the department/operational area or unit
- a schedule reference number
- reference numbers (if applicable) of the records
- descriptions of the record series/collections
- disposal action/retention period
- date of the schedule
- signatures of the Records Manager and Business Manager.

The Records Manager should maintain a master set of all schedules and amendments/additions must be agreed with him/her before updated versions are issued.

There are many types of record common to all organizations. These are commonly called 'generic' or 'housekeeping' records. Many of these were the first to be managed electronically (for example, financial and human resource records). These generic records probably account for as much as 50% of an organization's records. Whether they are in paper or electronic format, their retention periods should be the same – we are, of course, appraising the information not the medium. Several guidelines have been issued by different organizations covering the disposal of generic records in different sectors. Among the best are:

1 *Public sector*:
   The National Archives –
   www.nationalarchives.gov.uk/recordsmanagement/advice/schedules.htm
   Records Management Society – www.rms-gb.org.uk/resources/91
2 *Private sector*:
   Institute of Chartered Secretaries and Administrators (ICSA) –
   www.icsabookshop.co.uk/atozlisting.php

One of the dilemmas in applying disposal schedules in an electronic environment is how far aggregation should be applied. Given the nature of the records and the macro appraisal methodology that has to be applied, it seems sensible to base the scheduling at folder level. Any further granularity – to individual documents for example – would make the exercise excessively time consuming and resource intensive.

Transfer to an archive

Few archive repositories are yet in a position to accept electronic records for permanent preservation. In the UK The National Archives (TNA) are nearing the end of a long and ambitious programme called Seamless Flow. The programme involves the creation of a seamless flow of electronic records from creation in government departments, to preservation in the archives, through to delivery on the internet. The programme is about linking together existing components and automating manual processes. The process of developing the seamless-flow approach allows for the review and streamlining of other aspects of TNA architecture – notably catalogues and web searching. The development of an internet-based delivery system for digital records is a key component of the response to the UK Government's 'Modernising Government' target. [A core target in the UK's White Paper *Modernising Government* (CM 4310) stated, 'By the year 2004 all newly created public records will be electronically stored and retrieved.']

The Seamless Flow Programme is divided into a number of projects which progress according to an agreed programme plan. One of these projects is concerned with appraisal and another with transfer. The latter project aims to develop and implement processes for the transfer of electronic records and metadata from government departments to The National Archives and to specify, develop and implement a set of products that will automate where possible and appropriate all processes involved in transferring records from government departments to the point of loading to a pre-accession server. This project is at the heart of the programme. It is leading, and will lead, to many changes in business practices in government departments, and probably the wider public sector. For detailed information on the programme you should consult TNA's website www.nationalarchives.gov.uk/electronicrecords/seamless_flow/default.htm.

In the matter of the appraisal of electronic records and their transfer to an archive there may be specific procedures to undertake that have not been necessary in the paper environment. For example, if the archive undertakes to accession electronic records in their original form wherever possible, a technical report will need to be completed in sufficient detail for the evaluation of all the possible technical issues that may bar transfer. The report would alert the archive to potential problems relating to the storage, preservation or presentation of the records. It could also identify particular sets of records that are at risk, costs associated with transfer and potential access problems. Enquiries are likely to be made in the following areas:

- nature of the records
- details of the hardware, operating and software programme supporting the records
- file formats
- access restrictions
- data types (dynamic and passive files)
- storage medium
- volume
- quality of associated metadata
- existence and location of finding aids
- associated costs relating to maintaining the records collection.

So when you come to the stage of transferring electronic records to an archive, be prepared to address technical as well as intellectual issues.

Destruction

In practice, deleting an electronic record merely removes an operating system link or application link to the record. The record itself is not actually removed. Re-use by overwriting is an option but if the media contain sensitive information, total erasure or destruction may be necessary. When destroying restricted documents, especially those that are security classified, it is usually necessary to erase the entire disk or tape, in order to ensure that the file in question cannot be recovered.

Documenting appraisal

It is important to document appraisal decisions (see Table 7.2), for the following reasons:

Organizations need to maintain an audit trail of important decisions. In the case of public authorities in the UK, this is specified in the *Code of Practice on the Management of Records under the Freedom of Information Act 2000* (2002).

The archives institution must also be accountable for decisions about the permanent preservation of records that provide the historical accountability of the organization.

It may be policy (either now or in the future) to re-examine appraisal decisions to determine if a more appropriate decision can be made. Access to the reasoning behind the original decision is essential.

The research and analysis required to arrive at an appraisal decision can be of use for other purposes. In archival description, the documentation of appraisal decisions can provide vital information about the provenance of the records and may also help in the preparation of administrative histories and finding aids.

In essence the documentation of destruction of records must provide evidence that destruction has taken place in accordance with established policies and schedules. The kinds of documentation that might be kept are:

- acquisition policies
- selection policies
- disposal schedules
- record transfer lists and receipts
- record transfer or presentation agreements
- lists of records destroyed
- certificates of destruction.

Table 7.2 Sample table of requirements for retention and disposal

Ref	Requirement	M/HD/D*	Comments
2.1	The system must allow the allocation of a disposal or review schedule to each folder, sub-folder (or record) or to a group of folders and sub-folders.	M	
2.2	The system must allow the allocation of a disposal or review schedule to a specific folder or sub-folder that can take precedence over a schedule allocated at a higher hierarchical point of the file plan.	M	
2.3	The system must provide alerts to nominated users when disposals or reviews are scheduled to take place.	M	
2.4	The system must ensure that destroyed folders (or records) cannot be retrieved by use of any specialist recovery tools.	HD	
2.5	The system must allow for disposal schedules to be calculated against time, specific actions or a combination of both; for example, *three years after project end*.	M	
2.6	The system must support separate disposal instruction; for example, *further retention and review at a later date*; *transfer to an archive*; *destroy*.	M	
2.7	The system must not automatically destroy records that are referenced in other folders or sub-folders.	M	
2.8	The system must seek nominated user approval prior to the destruction of records.	M	
2.9	The system must be able to report on the disposal of records across the file plan, including destruction.	M	
2.10	The system must allow for notes/metadata to be added to folders relating to disposal schedules and reviews.	M	
2.11	The system must be capable of restricting the ability to allocate and amend disposal schedules to records managers.	M	

Continued on next page

Table 7.2 *Continued*

Ref	Requirement	M/HD/D*	Comments
2.12	The system must be able to export specific information (content and metadata) either selectively or in bulk, without degradation of content or format and without loss of any element of the record.	M	
2.13	The system should be able to support (for example, by interfacing with workflow facilities) the scheduling, review and export process by tracking their progress.	HD	
2.14	The system must produce a report in the event of any failure to export electronic records and associated metadata.	M	
2.15	The system must retain intact all electronic folders that have been exported at least until confirmation of a successful transfer process.	M	
2.16	The system should support the selection and export of metadata, independently of record content, in a form suitable for migration to a web-based environment in order to support a resource discovery service.	D	
2.17	The system should provide the ability to sort electronic folders selected for transfer into ordered lists according to user-defined metadata elements.	D	
2.18	The system should provide for the retention of metadata elements for folders, sub-folders and records that have been destroyed.	HD	

* M – mandatory; HD – highly desirable; D – desirable

These requirements are provided as a sample only. Organizations will have their own specific requirements based on their business processes and procedures as well as their business culture.

APPENDIX:

Appraisal report for records created in an electronic records management system

(Reproduced with kind permission from the National Weights and Measures Laboratory)

Name of organization

National Weights and Measures Laboratory (NWML) www.nwml.gov.uk/default.asp

What type of agency is the organization?

Executive Agency	Non-Departmental Public Body	Trading Fund	Next Steps Agency	Non-Ministerial bodies	Libraries, Museums, Galleries	Research Councils
*						

Sources of Information:

- www.civil-service.co.uk/index.asp
- Organization

What is the annual budget of the organization?

2004: operating costs were 3.2m. But funding from DTI = £640,000, rest of income to come from services provided.

What is the total number of employees?

50

Background, functions and activities

NWML has been an Executive Agency of the Department of Trade and Industry since 1989. It was formerly the Standards Department of the Board of Trade and successor departments. It is the focus for legal metrology in the UK.

NWML champions innovation and excellence through fair, accurate and legal measurement. It supports the importance of an infrastructure provided by a legal weights and measures system in the UK as a basis for competitive markets and consumer protection locally, nationally and internationally.
NWML's principal activities are:

- Maintenance of national measurement standards
- Preparation of secondary legislation (SIs under Weights and Measures Act 1965 and European Communities Act 1972)
- Presentation of national viewpoint on legal metrology in the EC (WELMEC) and internationally (OIML)
- Ensuring, by a system of design type assessment and approval, that weighing and measuring equipment for trade complies with UK Regulations or EC Directives
- Provision of a calibration and equipment testing service
- Provision of quality management certification through an accredited certification body
- Provision of training and consultancy services in legal metrology.

Sources of information:

- Annual report and accounts
- Framework document.

Name of the parent or sponsoring organization

(If none, which Minister lays an annual report before Parliament?)
Department of Trade and Industry.

Relationship with parent department

DTI determines the policy framework within which NWML operates but is not involved in the day-to-day management. NWML maintains a close working relationship with DTI as most of its work forms part of a *programme* funded by the Department's *National Measurement System Policy Unit* (NMSPU). In this way NWML acts as a contractor for the DTI in ensuring that the milestones in the work programme are met. It has been a net running cost Agency since 1996. Responsibility for NWML currently lies with the Consumer and Competition Policy Division in the Innovation Group of DTI.

Is the Agency involved in the instigation and/or development of primary legislation?

No

Areas of policy work undertaken in the Agency

Type of policy	Yes/No	Notes
All policy is made in parent department	Yes	Most of NWML's work forms part of a *programme* funded by the Department's *National Measurement System Policy Unit* (NMSPU) Policy in the form of standards made in NWML DTI programmes are easily located within the file plan
Agency plays major consultative role in the development of policy	No	But plays a major role in consultation on standards, their operation and their implementation
Agency represents the parent department/UK govt at international conferences/on European or International bodies	Yes	NWML represents the UK in discussions about European and International harmonization of legal metrology and implementation of EU directives. Provides secretariat/chairs for bodies or technical committees. NWML tends to drive forward EU directives. Records of this work are in the International section of the file plan
Agency develops operational policy only	Yes	Main policy undertaken takes the form of standards published as SIs and guidance to accompany them

Is any policy development captured through case files and databases?

No

Summary of the operational work undertaken by the agency

Operational activity		Type of record created	Is the work captured through a database?	Is the work captured through publications (see below)?	Do appeals go elsewhere (parent dept, independent panel)?	Are key results captured in the Annual Report?
Licensing	N					
Monitoring	N					
Inspecting and verification within a legal framework	Y	Reports – Local authorities are inspected on 5 year cycles to have standards re-verified	No	No	N/A	No
Inspecting and verification outside a legal framework	N					
Setting industry standards	Y	SIs, Regs, Codes of Practice and Guidance Notes	No	Yes	N/A	Only performance against targets
Providing training/skills	Y	Course materials	No	No	N/A	No
Handling complaints	N					
Testing, approving, accrediting industry products and/or organizations	Y	Approvals for types of weighing and measuring instruments, for calibrations and notified bodies are provided in the form of certificates	Yes PADS and EMeTAS. All databases now in ERMS	No	N/A	Only performance against targets
Providing a service to another department or organization, e.g. local authorities, industry, car service, defence agencies?	Y	Through above, also provides traceability, certification to ISO 9001 standards, testing and auditing for National Lottery	No	No	N/A	No
Making payments in response to applications	N					
Providing guidance, information and support	Y	Leaflets, guidance notes	No	Yes	N/A	No
Supervising organizations	Y	Reports	No	No	N/A	No

What publications does the organization regularly produce?

Types of publications	Place or form of publication	Preservation strategy
Standards	SIs – HMSO	To be checked
Inspections	Not published	
Guidance/ codes of practice	Published – some on web	To be checked
Training manuals, curricula	Not published	
Annual reports	Web, HMSO	Send to TNA
Research reports	None	
Main output is public information, e.g. museums, archives	Specialized information for customers	To be checked
Trade journals		

Sources of information are:

- Agency website
- Parent organization website
- TNA catalogue: http://na-nt-web1/Reader/default.asp
- DRO

Material transferred to The National Archives in the past

Underlinings show references to series in The National Archives.

Records of the Standards, Weights and Measures Departments 1829–1984

Records of the Standards, Weights and Measures Departments of the Board of Trade and successors. relating to the verification of standards and the advising of other governments using the same standards.

The main correspondence and papers of the department are in BT 101 with files in the STD series relating to legislation, testing and inspection and metrication in BT 290 and files in the SM series relating to the changeover to the metric system in FV 40.

Selected reports by inspectors of weights and measures, for 1952 and from 1957 onwards, are in BT 184

Registers of candidates for Weights and Measures Inspectorate examinations are in BT 312 (no records transferred)

Schedules of statistics extracted from annual reports of Local Weights and Measures Authorities are in BT 313 (no records transferred)

Appraisal hypothesis

Databases created by NWML consist only of certificates and test approvals giving information about the name of the product and whether it has passed various tests. *These have no long-term historical value.*

Policy is mainly made in the DTI. NWML represents the UK in Europe and internationally and plays an important role there. These organizations (OIML and WELMEC) aim to establish harmonization and mutual co-operation in legal metrology. WELMEC is not an EU body – it is a voluntary body set up by EU and EFTA countries to gain European co-operation in legal metrology. However, the outcome of NWML participation will be reflected in the standards and guidance. *Policy and meetings files have no long-term historical value.*

Standards for products, measures and calibration are provided through publications.

We would expect in such circumstances to preserve only board minutes and papers, annual reports.

However, some areas of operational policy may be of long-term historical interest, namely:

- Trial of the Pyx – *documented in Royal Mint and Exchequer records*
- Legal enforcement cases: metric martyrs, froth on beer . . . there may be others *handled by local trading standards departments*
- Harmonization – *check policy area and minutes of committees. Select latter in preference*
- Privatization – NWML was a candidate for this and the issue continues to hover – *covered in Steering Board records*
- Development of international customers – *covered in Executive Committee records*
- Relationship with DTI may be important to document. *This can be done quite easily through preservation of the DTI programmes (copy and outcomes only).*

Are the selection suggestions above in line with any Operational Selection Policies?

Yes

Check of records has been completed as below:

Board papers
Steering Board – composition and remit

There are four non-executive members of the Steering Board, three members from DTI and the Chief Executive of NWML. The Steering Board considers the Agency's forward strategic plan and priorities, high-level objectives and targets and new ways of working. It provides guidance on the operation of and development of NWML but has no executive role.

Steering Board – policies and strategies considered
Agencies review, Hampton review, Scoping study on future, Corporate and Business Plan, development of new business, policy on commercial work, Measuring Instruments Directive (MID) – progress, finance, governance, re-organization, DTI programme

Physical check – information quality			
Agenda			
Papers			
Minutes			

Executive Team – composition and remit

The team comprises the Chief Executive and the Directors. Its function is to produce a long-term business strategy to ensure a successful business which meets the requirements and needs of NWML's stakeholders. The Executive Team replaced the Strategy Team in April 2004.

Executive Team – policies and strategies considered
Service delivery, customer and stakeholder activities, new markets and services, regulatory and international, finance

Physical check – information quality			
Agenda			
Papers			
Minutes			

Annual report

Activity	Coverage
Operational	Performance against targets – financial, efficiency, throughput, customer satisfaction and growth – mainly time based
Provision of services	Progress and issues
Customers and stakeholders	Progress and issues
Organizational structure	Chart and update
Future plans	Update

DTI programme

Programme milestones	
Programme outcomes	

TNA records

Weights and Measures Inspectors reports (BT 184) – last record 1975

Information content	
TNA	To be checked
Current	To be checked

Impact on records of parent department

None

Implications for appraisal of agency's paper records

To be addressed

This paper should be submitted to a panel of client managers/RRP so that a collegiate view can be reached and consistency with other appraisals monitored. There should be a summary of the actual records to be selected together with any additional information and (if possible) suggestions on how the selections can be applied to the Agency's paper records also.

Preservation

This chapter covers the storage and preservation of electronic records, examining the procedures that need to be considered in both the medium term (sustainability) and long term (preservation). It also provides pointers to the technical help that may be required when undertaking this phase of the design process. It also looks at business continuity planning for electronic records.

Sustainability/preservation

'Sustainability' is often used in electronic records management to cover those records and their metadata that require continued retention by the creating or owning organization until such time as they can be destroyed or transferred to an archive for permanent preservation. 'Preservation', on the other hand, is generally used to cover those records which have passed out of the custody of the creating or owning organization because they no longer have any active use for them and which have been passed to another organization where they will either be preserved permanently or destroyed. The descriptions might therefore be applied to electronic records in the medium term and long term respectively, but for the purposes of this book and for simplification, preservation will be used to cover both.

Why do we need a preservation strategy?

There is a growing realization that future access to electronic information is threatened. It is perhaps surprising that this has not come about before now. Part of this can be put down to commonly adopted policies and procedures to maintain information in paper form even though much of it has been created electronically. There is still a certain amount of distrust of electronically preserved information. People feel more at home with paper and, in the absence of overall strategies on the management and preservation of electronic records, they have continued in this comfort zone. Another factor has been the concentration on earlier phases of the life cycle of records – developing systems for the creation and management of current records – and on delivering services to the public electronically. However, over the past few years, as the technology has become more robust, reliable and (most important) secure, many sectors have developed strategies for maintaining and preserving their information resources solely in electronic form. As these strategies are maturing – many are now five or more years old – the question of preservation of the 'born-digital' information has become a vital issue. For example, in the central government sector in 1999 the White Paper *Modernising Government* (Cm 4310, March 1999) made the statement that '. . . It is our aim that by the year 2004 all newly-created public records will be electronically stored and retrieved.' Not every single government department was able to introduce electronic records management systems in accordance with this aim, but enough did so to now find themselves having to contemplate changes to, or upgrades of, their systems and to think seriously about preservation issues. The National Archives' Seamless Flow Programme (described on page 117) was partly introduced to respond to that situation.

When we spoke of 'long-term' preservation in the paper records environment, we probably meant 25 years or more. In the electronic environment it is more likely to be 5–7 years; long term usually means 'greater than one generation of technology'. After that period of time new versions of software are available, new technology has created new and better systems, and the storage medium itself may have changed. (Remember five and a quarter inch floppy disks and three and a half inch disks? These were the standard not so long ago, but are all now superseded by compact discs.)

Many records have retention periods greater than one generation of technology. It is important that these records are preserved and made accessible. They may be required for a number of purposes:

- daily business
- supporting strategic planning and decision making
- meeting legal requirements
- corporate (archival) memory.

Challenges and issues

The challenges involved in maintaining access to electronic records relate closely to the differences between the management of paper records and electronic records. For example:

- The media on which most electronic records are stored are fragile and inherently unstable; without suitable storage conditions they will deteriorate.
- Electronic records are machine dependent, requiring specific hardware and software to make them accessible.

- Changes can potentially be made to electronic records with ease which means that the essential characteristics of a record (as defined by the international standard Records Management ISO 15489) – authenticity, reliability, integrity and usability – increase in importance.
- Prioritizing the preservation of electronic records is of the greatest importance since, if early preservation is not applied, the information may be lost.
- The preservation of electronic records requires new skills and closer co-operation with specialists.
- New organizational structures may be required to support electronic preservation.
- Issues of copyright and similar rights regarding electronic information are still to be finalized.
- There is a huge increase in the amount of information created and greater interest on the part of researchers in accessing it.

All these issues mean that there has to be a very different approach to the preservation of electronic records from that used for paper records. Preservation action must be planned and implemented at regular intervals and, as far as possible, automated. In order to achieve the goals of preservation, organizations require an appropriate level of functionality together with the tools and procedures required to support it. It will be necessary to preserve electronic records over time as a corporate asset, in a manner that retains their reliability and integrity for as long as they are required. This will also include prevention of changes to content and context (so that authenticity is retained) and continued maintenance in an appropriate format (so that accessibility is retained).

Authenticity

ISO 15489 states that:

An authentic record is one that can be proven

a) to be what it purports to be
b) to have been created or sent by the person purported to have created or sent it, and
c) to have been created or sent at the time purported

To ensure the authenticity of records, organizations should implement and document policies and procedures which control the creation, receipt, transmission, maintenance and disposition of records to ensure that record creators are authorized and identified and that records are protected against unauthorized addition, deletion, alteration, use and concealment.

A presumption of authenticity can be made from the number of requirements that have been met and the degree to which each has been met – the higher the number satisfied and the greater the degree to which an individual requirement has been satisfied, the stronger the presumption of authenticity. The National Archives has published generic requirements for sustaining electronic information over time; these can be seen at www.nationalarchives.gov.uk/electronicrecords/ reqs_sustain.htm.

Reliability

ISO 15489 regards a reliable record as one 'whose contents can be trusted as a full and accurate representation of transactions, activities or facts to which they attest and can be depended upon in the course of subsequent transactions or activities'. It continues:

> Any system deployed to manage records should be capable of continuous and regular operation in accordance with responsible procedures. A records system should
>
> * Routinely capture all records within the scope of the business activities it covers
> * Organize the records in a way that reflects the business processes of the record's creator
> * Protect the records from unauthorised alteration or disposition
> * Routinely function as the primary source of information about actions that are documented in the records, and
> * Provide ready access to all relevant records and related metadata.

Reliability will therefore be apparent if there is evidence that the records were created and captured as part of a legitimate business process and assigned to a logical and appropriate location within the organization's file plan.

Integrity

ISO 15489 states that:

> The integrity of a record refers to its being complete and unaltered. . . . Control measures such as access monitoring, user verification, authorised destruction and security controls should be implemented to prevent unauthorised access, destruction, alteration or removal of records. These controls may reside within a records system or be external to the specific system. For electronic records the organization may need to provide that any system malfunction, upgrade or regular maintenance does not affect the records.

If we need to confirm that a record is unchanged or that only authorized and appropriate changes have been made, the status of the records and the presence or absence of change has to be auditable.

Usability

ISO 15489 defines a usable record as 'one that can be located, retrieved, presented and interpreted'. These aspects may vary according to business need. There may be other uses required of the record/information than that of the operational process that created it. For example it may be necessary to provide access in different forms linked to records created subsequently.

Planning for preservation

Technology watch

Much of the pain associated with preservation strategies can be avoided if proper plans for such issues as obsolescent technology are made in the first place. Organizations need to ensure that electronic records that need to be retained can be copied, reformatted, converted or migrated across successive generations of hardware and software. Consider, for example:

- how long is proprietary software likely to be available?
- what is the cost of maintaining access to obsolete formats and systems?
- what is the likely life of the medium on which electronic information is being stored?
- how long will operating systems be available?

These requirements are generally grouped under the heading of 'technology watch'. A technology watch programme will need to monitor software and hardware environments and establish procedures to determine what action should be taken when it is considered that hardware, software or storage media are obsolescent.

Managing preservation

Organizations should also establish a management framework – comprising policies, processes and people – to deal with preservation issues. It is all very well having a preservation strategy but how is it going to be carried through, who will undertake the necessary tasks and how will its effectiveness be measured? The key tasks for such an undertaking will include:

- identifying the records that need to be preserved and for how long
- determining how the implementation of preservation techniques will be documented
- determining how the preserved records will continue to satisfy the four characteristics of authenticity, reliability, integrity and usability
- determining the roles, responsibilities and resources required to implement the strategy

- communicating preservation information inside and outside the organization
- integrating the strategy within performance measurement procedures
- making reference to legal obligations affecting preservation (for example, legal admissibility of electronic information).

Standards

There are several standards and best practice guidelines that are relevant to the preservation of electronic records. Some of these are sector-specific. You should take into account the following:

BS 7799 (ISO 27001) and ISO 17799, Information security management

The full title of ISO 17799 is Information technology, Security techniques, Code of practice for information security management. The current standard is a revision of that published in 2000, which was identical to the British Standard BS 7799 (Part 1). It provides best-practice recommendations on information security management, which is defined as 'the preservation of confidentiality (ensuring that information is accessible only to those authorized to have access), integrity (safeguarding the accuracy and completeness of information and processing methods) and availability (ensuring that authorized users have access to information and associated assets when required'.) The recommendations include risk assessments, security policy, asset management, physical and environmental security, access control and business continuity management. The second part of BS 7799 described the basis for an assessment of an organization's information security management system; when it was internationalized in 2005 it became ISO 27001.

BIP 0008, Code of practice for legal admissibility and evidential weight of information stored electronically

This Code of Practice is primarily concerned with the authenticity, integrity and availability of electronically communicated information. The code seeks to define operational procedures which comply with 'good practice' in the field of electronic document communications.

e-Government Interoperability Framework (e-GIF)

e-GIF defines the technical policies and specifications governing information flows across the UK government and public sector. These cover interconnectivity, data integration, access and content management. Some of the key e-GIF policies are:

- Adoption of common specifications used on the internet and world wide web

for all public-sector information systems
- Adoption of XML as the primary standard for data integration and presentation tools
- Adoption of browser-based technology
- Development and adoption of the e-Government Metadata Standard (e-GMS), which is based on the Dublin Core
- Development and maintenance of IPSV – the Integrated Public Sector Vocabulary.

Open Archival Information System (OAIS)

The OAIS is a conceptual framework rather than a prescriptive standard; it is intended to identify the necessary features of an archival information system rather than to recommend any particular information. Nevertheless it can be extremely useful in developing preservation strategies. The model is set in the context of creators, users and managers of information. It recognizes three variants of information package – a package being something that includes both the record object and metadata (which includes preservation description information – a history of the content, context, references and checksums, etc. to monitor degradation or alteration). The three packages are:

- Archival Information Package (AIP) – the package that the system actually preserves
- Submission Information Package (SIP) – how information is submitted to the OAIS; it may be structured differently from the AIP and contain insufficient preservation data
- Dissemination Information Package (DIP) – versions of the AIP which are tailored to user requirements.

The main functions of an OAIS are:

- ingest – the incorporation of submitted information into the preservation system/archive
- archival storage – the storage of the AIPs
- data management
- administration
- preservation planning – ensuring that policies and procedures in place adequately protect the system from technological changes
- access – the search and retrieval of archived information.

Developing the preservation strategy

The strategy itself will need to list categories, volumes and formats of the records that have been identified for preservation treatment, identify the mechanisms to be used and apply preservation considerations to new collections of records as they are created or identified.

Preservation options

1 *Native format on existing platforms* – maintaining electronic records in the current software format on the existing hardware platform. This is really only an option if the information in the records is required for a short time – only, say, two or three years. Even then it depends on whether the organization can maintain the relevant hardware and make available relevant versions of the software (including the appropriate licence).

2 *Managing the storage media* – early approaches to electronic records preservation relied on storing records in their original format on physical media, such as magnetic tape, optical disks, compact discs (CD) and digital versatile discs (DVD). These media, however, have been designed for short-term storage of information. After a relatively short period of time it is unlikely that the hardware and software will be available to access the records. In addition, the media themselves may physically deteriorate.

If this method of preservation is chosen for some records, there are some useful points to bear in mind. When choosing the media, for example, choose one that is in a standard format and that has, as far as possible, a predictable life span. Select media that have had substantial take-up in the information management and ICT professions and balance the cost of your choice against the value and retention time of the records that you are storing. Bear in mind the environmental conditions that are required to store the media. Regarding temperature and humidity, the British Standard BS 4783 recommendations are shown in Table 8.1.

Table 8.1 Recommended temperature and relative humidity levels

Device	Operating	Non-operating	Long term
Magnetic tape reel, 12.7mm	18 to 24° C 40 to 60% RH	5 to 32° C 20 to 80% RH	18 to 22° C 35 to 45% RH
Magnetic tape cassettes, 12.7mm	18 to 24° C 45 to 55% RH	5 to 32° C 5 to 80% RH	18 to 22° C 35 to 45% RH
Magnetic tape cartridges	10 to 45° C 20 to 80% RH	5 to 45° C 20 to 80% RH	18 to 22° C 35 to 45% RH
Magnetic tape – 4 & 8mm helical scan	5 to 45° C 20 to 80% RH	5 to 45° C 20 to 80% RH	5 to 32° C 20 to 60% RH
Optical disk cartridges (ODC)	10 to 50° C 18 to 80% RH	-10 to 50° C 5 to 90% RH	18 to 22° C 35 to 45% RH
CD-ROM	10 to 50° C 10 to 80% RH	-10 to 50° C 5 to 90% RH	18 to 22° C 35 to 45% RH

In addition:

- avoid ultra-violet light, chemicals, mould and dust
- keep in closed metal cabinets and avoid magnetic fields
- reduce handling to a minimum
- pack media securely.

Keep a record of the number of times the media are accessed since this can affect their longevity. Make regular checks of the media to search for signs of decay and consider whether the data needs to be copied to new media or even migrated (see below).

3 *Manage the format* – if you can tell that certain record collections are going to be kept for longer than two or three years, you might consider choosing a format at the outset that would be more suitable for such storage. Choice of file format should always be determined by the functional requirements of the record-creating process. As we have seen, long-term preservation might be a requirement both for ongoing business processes and archival preservation. Costs are inevitably minimized when these factors are taken into account prior to record creation – attempts to bring electronic records into a managed and sustainable regime after the fact tend to be expensive, complex and, generally, less successful. The National Archives have produced detailed guidance on selecting file formats which, rather than repeat here, can be accessed on their website: www.nationalarchives.gov.uk/preservation/advice/digital.htm.

You may also find it useful to look at the e-Government Interoperability Framework (e-GIF). This defines the technical policies and specifications governing information flows across government and the public sector. These cover interconnectivity, data integration, e-services access and content management. Version 6.1 contains the high-level policy statements, management, implementation and compliance regimes, and lists many appropriate formats. See the website www.govtalk.gov.uk/schemasstandards/egif.asp.

4 *Migration* – the transformation of data from one format to another or from an earlier version to a current version of the same format. It is performed by a set of customized programmes or scripts that automatically transfer the data. Migration aims to retain the ability to display, retrieve, manipulate and use digital information in the face of constantly changing technology. It involves changing its configuration and format and there may be some loss of the original representation. Upgrading systems in this way is normally only done on current records, not on semi-current records or archives. If migration is carried out in an unmanaged way, valuable records could be lost forever. There are a few aspects to be borne in mind when considering migration:

- If records are maintained in a proprietary format, migration may prove difficult if the supplier no longer supports the relevant format or is no longer in business. Frequent monitoring of the market place should enable you to keep in touch with developments in this area and thus help you to plan migration in advance of any such difficulties (see Technology watch, page 133). It is a common experience to have to migrate some office applications after as little as three years.

- Migration can sometimes lead to loss of some characteristics of the original format. It may be wise to undertake a risk assessment to judge whether some loss of functionality might be acceptable. In addition, checks may need to be made that no information has been lost in the process.
- Should you try to guard against some of the disadvantages of migration by preserving original files (as well as the migrated files)? Again a risk assessment might be the way forward here to see whether such preservation is cost effective.
- Migration should always support business needs as well as preserve record content. You may therefore not want to contemplate migrating to a format that cannot be searched or copied.
- Consider whether migration to XML (Extensible Mark-up Language) is viable. XML provides a universal, standardized and well supported mechanism for marking up data for use on the internet or in other applications.
- Compliance with the *Code of Practice for Legal Admissibility and Evidential Weight of Information Stored Electronically (BIP 0008)* may be an important issue.
- Back-up copies of the records will need to be checked to ensure that they are up to date as far as use and availability are concerned.
- If a formal migration strategy is adopted, it must be integrated with corporate management policies and procedures. There must be clearly defined roles, responsibilities, targets and monitoring.
- The process of migration must be authenticated and documented.

5 *Emulation* – the development of software/hardware combinations to replicate the behaviour of obsolete processes. They may include interfaces, operating systems or hardware configurations. The replication enables electronic information using obsolete systems to be accessed by modern systems. Emulation requires that the appropriate software has to be provided on every system that might need access to the preserved files or, at the very least, on one system that might require physical access. Either way it could be an expensive option since it needs highly skilled computer programmers to write the necessary code.

Databases

The preservation of databases may require some special attention. You will need to distinguish between those elements of the database that require preservation and those that will not, and this will depend on the type of system. For example, in some databases old information is overwritten by new information while in others information is never removed or overwritten. Some databases have no time restrictions – information is collected and analysed on a regular basis but the system is not closed down until it is succeeded by a new system or decommissioned completely; others, such as those collecting information as part of a survey, are designed to record a specific set of information and then closed. Clearly, the nature of some databases will not allow a choice of what information within it can be preserved – it will be a question of all or nothing. However, some organizations and archive establishments like to take snapshots of databases – a copy of all data in the system at some instant in time taken periodically. The result is usually converted to a standard form rather than kept in its native form. Other organizations, feeling that the snapshot procedure alone does not adequately capture the information flow through a system (it will show, for example, how many cases were dealt with at the time but not how many are dealt with every year, month, etc.), will preserve the audit trail with the snapshot – information about every alteration made to records in the system.

Business continuity

Planning for business continuity and disaster recovery is a key element of the preservation strategy. There are regulations in both public and private sectors that give statutory force to the requirement of organizations to deal with the likely risks that face them. You will see various statistics on business continuity websites that illustrate the consequences of the absence of such planning. For example, only 20% of organizations without a business continuity plan are likely to survive; 90% of organizations that suffer a significant data loss are not in business two years later. Business continuity planning covers the policies and procedures for the development, testing and maintenance of plans that enable an organization to continue to operate during and after a disaster. Disaster recovery planning is usually a part of the business continuity framework; it focuses on the recovery of specific operations, functions, services and applications (like records).

Business continuity is not just an ICT issue. Loss of physical premises, machinery, equipment and paper records are all possible continuity risks. There is a British Standard that describes best practice on business continuity – BS 25999. It is based on the business continuity planning life cycle, as illustrated in Figure 8.1.

The standard takes the form of guidance and recommendations, and establishes the process, principles and terminology of business continuity management.

Another good guide was produced by the former Cabinet Office agency Property Advisers to the Civil Estate (PACE). It is still available at: www.ogc.gov.uk/documents/PACE_-_BCPG.pdf.

Figure 8.1 The business continuity planning life cycle

Requirements

A sample table of requirements is given in the Appendix at the end of this chapter.

Implementing the preservation strategy

There is no substitute for good preparation for preservation. All the work you invest in research and planning will make implementation much easier. There are a number of key steps that you should undertake to implement the strategy:

1   Work closely with business managers to identify those electronic records that the organization wants to preserve for continued business use. In view of the expense that preservation will incur, this needs to be an appropriately robust procedure. Many local business managers and operators will quite naturally contend that their information must be available beyond five years or after their systems change. Very often this contention is in the nature of a safety blanket, and on closer examination you may find that they can often manage (sometimes more effectively) without out-of-date information. You might take the line of suggesting that the cost of preservation is borne by their budgets.

2   Work closely with archivists to decide which electronic records will be selected for permanent preservation. Ensure that agreed appraisal procedures are undertaken and that selected records are dealt with in a timely manner. Digital preservation solutions are increasingly being introduced by national and local archive organizations. In the UK The National Archives' Seamless Flow programme is addressing the appraisal, transfer, preservation and presentation of central government records. In 2001 the Digital Preservation

Coalition (DPC) was established to foster joint action to address the urgent challenges of securing the preservation of digital resources in the UK and to work with others internationally to secure global digital memory and knowledge bases.

3 Decide which preservation approach your organization will undertake. Will it be the same for all types of records or will certain categories of records be dealt with differently from the most common procedure? For example, you may wish to keep records to which you only require infrequent access in the medium term on CDs while others which you use on a frequent and regular basis will need to be migrated to new systems.

4 Work closely with ICT staff to examine the technical solutions that need to be used to ensure that your preferred approach is successfully implemented. This may, for example, involve the writing of new metadata or even the development of specialized software.

5 Identify the personnel in your organization who will actually undertake the preservation process. Will it be existing ICT staff or are you going to buy in the expertise in the form of consultants/contractors? Examine the many dependent issues in making the decision such as the sensitivity of the records or the added costs.

6 Test the procedures which you have decided upon. It would be preferable to undertake these tests on copies of records. This stage may lead to a re-examination of procedures and changes in approach. This step should also include verification that all relevant legal obligations regarding the information in the records have been met.

7 As a security measure you should make a temporary back-up of all those records that are going to be preserved until the preservation process has proven successful. The back-ups will need to meet the requirements of authenticity, reliability and integrity. They can be destroyed once you are satisfied with the preservation solution.

8 Undertake the preservation process. Ensure that adequate documentation and metadata are kept.

9 Verify that the process has been successful – that functionality, content, format and structure have been retained within acceptable limits. The business managers of the areas in which the records were created or are used should be closely involved at this stage. If the process proves to be unsuccessful, then it should be repeated. A further failure may lead to a reassessment of the preservation procedures themselves and perhaps the application of a different method.

10 When all interested parties are satisfied that the preservation has been carried out successfully and that the records are usable, authentic and reliable, the original records can be destroyed. There should, incidentally, be some authority for this. Typically, an entry on disposal schedules will have been agreed – for example, *electronic records which have been migrated to a new format; destroy*

six months after migration.

11 Maintain communication and monitoring procedures on all aspects of preservation in accordance with corporate performance management regimes.

Taking preservation forward

The volume and complexity of electronic resources to be preserved will continue to increase rapidly over the next few years. Most members of the information management profession are agreed that there is an urgent need to develop expertise on a shared service basis to ensure the long-term preservation of our vital information resources. Currently, some of the best advice and guidance can be found from the Digital Preservation Coalition (www.dpconline.org/graphics/index.html) and from the Digital Preservation Department of The National Archives (www.nationalarchives. gov.uk/preservation/digital.htm).

APPENDIX
Sample table of requirements for preservation

Ref	Requirement	M/HD/D*	Comments
3.1	The system must use storage media that explicitly meet industry standards	M	
3.2	The system must provide evidence of the degree of scalability that it can support over time, as organizational needs change and develop	M	
3.3	The system must include documentation and information on its capacity to store and export/import electronic objects and metadata	M	
3.4	The system must support the management of the storage of electronic objects and metadata across a range of media	M	
3.5	The system must be capable of backing up the electronic objects and metadata	M	
3.6	The system must support the duplication/replication of electronic objects and metadata between different storage media	M	
3.7	The system should maintain at least two copies of each electronic object and its metadata	HD	
3.8	If the system uses a combination of storage devices, they should be integrated to provide a seamless operation	HD	
3.9	The system must be able to provide management reports to support scalability and storage operations (for example, disposal rates, unavailable storage within the system and capacity threshold)	M	

Continued on next page

Continued from previous page

Ref	Requirement	M/HD/D*	Comments
3.10	The system must support the entry and storage of technical data about file formats and make it available as part of the organization's preservation planning procedures	M	
3.11	The system must alert that capacity thresholds are being approached	M	
3.12	The system must integrate with external software applications or checking procedures for verifying the integrity of storage media	M	
3.13	The production code of the system must meet the security requirements of any relevant security authority	M	
3.14	The system should be capable of linking with relevant software that is capable of producing redacted versions of records	D	
3.15	The system must be able to meet the management requirements of ISO 17799	M	
3.16	The system must be able to meet relevant interoperability requirements in respect of specified preservation procedures	M	
3.17	The system must support the migration of electronic objects prior to the technology by which they are managed becoming obsolete	M	
3.18	In the case of migration actions being reported as unsuccessful, the system should present options to rectify the errors	D	
3.19	The system must automatically produce a migration validation report	M	
3.20	The system should be able to record details in the audit trail of all viewings of record content, including the object viewed, the time and the identity of the user	HD	
3.21	The system must be able to maintain the links between the electronic objects, their metadata and the arrangement of the records according to the file plan	M	

* M – mandatory; HD – highly desirable; D – desirable

Access

This chapter briefly examines the subject of access in the context of electronic records – in particular accessibility, usability and security. While the basic principles are the same as those for paper records, there are some aspects that need particular attention when designing electronic records management systems. One of these is the redaction of electronic records and this subject is discussed in some detail.

General context

Public access to the records of public authorities is a fundamental right in a democratic society, but in the private sector access is usually restricted to people working for the particular business and, in some cases, to its shareholders. In general, access principles should focus on ensuring that the users of records and archives are clear about their rights and responsibilities. These may be enshrined in legislation – primary or secondary – or in policy statements. Ironically, in most of these cases access is actually about restrictions on access. For example, the UK Freedom of Information Act 2000 has one section providing a statutory right of access to information from public authorities and 23 sections of exemptions to that right; Companies Acts restrict access to certain types of information; and privacy legislation will allow you to see your own personal records but not those of anyone else.

There is, of course, a strong relationship between preservation and access. A major objective of preserving electronic records and information is to make them accessible for future generations. In the electronic environment it is usually beneficial to make preservation and access decisions at the same time. For example, there may be good technical and pragmatic reasons to separate an access copy of an electronic record from a preservation copy when it passes from active use. As we saw when discussing preservation issues, new manifestations of electronic objects will need to be made as systems change or are upgraded. The deposited object may need to be kept for audit or legal reasons.

Accessibility

Records and information are made available for three main reasons:

* to meet statutory, regulatory or litigation requirements (broadly defined as accountability)
* for business reasons (operational)
* to meet the research needs of other parties, usually the public (social).

The organization should have a user-management policy or access policy statement, setting out how user accounts and privileges are created, managed and deleted.

From a technical point of view, how are you going to provide access generally to the electronic file plan? Will you use a system of passwords for sections of the file plan or will you rely on the allocation of users to one or more user roles. The latter is currently the much preferred option, leaving passwords and user identifiers for initial access to computer systems and networks.

At the functional level of access there are several roles:

* system administrator
* local administrators
* records managers
* end users
* super users
* custodians.

The *system administrator* has global powers over the electronic records management application. He/she will be able to change user profiles, define and maintain available access control markings, and be able to configure the access control system to suit the business requirements of the organization.

A *local administrator* may have powers similar to a system administrator or records manager but only covering a small part of the file plan.

The *records manager* is responsible for implementing the electronic records management system in terms of its file plan, disposal schedules and access control system. These responsibilities may also include activities such as the maintenance of naming conventions and metadata encoding schemes.

End users, in the context of access, search for, capture and retrieve records from the system. There may be a variety of roles in this category. For example, a line manager in a finance department might be allocated to the following role: *View all folder descriptions in that part of the file plan under the function 'Finance'* and *Have access to all 'Finance' folders except those with a protective marking of Secret or above.* The Director of Finance, however, may be given a role that gives access to all folders under 'Finance' and be able to see folder descriptions for the whole of the file plan.

In general it is desirable for all records and metadata to be visible and retrievable by all users unless there is a specific reason for them not to be so (personal information, protective marking, etc.). If this were not the case, it would eliminate one of the benefits of electronic records management that we identified in the business plan – the promotion of the system as a corporate resource. However, an extension of this is the question whether all users should be allowed to create folders as well as the normal practice of capturing records in them. This might be possible if you were confident that all users are fully aware and familiar with records management principles and practices and with the structure and rationale of the file plan. Sadly, this is not often the case and the allocation of roles in the system might therefore include a *super user* – someone in each business area, working closely with the records manager, who will authorize the creation of folders for their particular area.

In some electronic records management systems *custodians* of certain folders may be allocated; this is typical where there may be high-level security markings and closer control of the ability to allocate and amend those markings is required.

Procedures should be established for electronic records management systems that ensure users' access rights are adjusted appropriately and in a timely manner whenever there is a change in business need, or if a user changes roles or leaves the organization. Procedures for the registration and deregistration of users and for managing access to all information management systems will need to be established to ensure that all users' access rights match their authorizations. For example, user access rights should be reviewed at regular intervals. These procedures would normally be the responsibility of the system administrator, or at least someone suitably trained and qualified, but the organization's (electronic) records manager should be a part of the scheme's management.

The electronic records management system will need to support a protective marking system that allocates security categories to records and folders. This protective marking system can be defined by the organization. In the UK government the following scheme is typical:

- Restricted
- Confidential – with sub-categories of
  — Confidential, staff
  — Confidential, management
  — Confidential, finance, etc.
- Secret
- Top secret.

As far as public use is concerned, public authorities (in the UK) must have in place procedures to deal with requests for information under the Freedom of Information Act 2000. A significant difference in applying FOI from access procedures in force before the legislation is that the FOI Act provides for access to information rather than records. This can have major implications for electronic records if it means that some need to be redacted before information is released.

Redaction

The Freedom of Information Act 2000, which came fully into effect on 1 January 2005, emphasizes the statutory right of access to information, rather than documents or records. Whereas in the past, if any document contained sensitive material, it was common to withhold the whole document from public inspection, it is now necessary for public authorities to consider the release of as much information as possible from a document, even if that means splitting the material up. The Lord Chancellor's Code of Practice on the Management of Records under Freedom of Information, issued under section 46 of the Act, states that where a complete document cannot be made available 'Authorities should consider whether parts of records might be released if the sensitive information were blanked out'.

Redaction has therefore become an important and sensitive issue since the introduction of Freedom of Information. While important principles have been established in the paper environment, some modification has to be made to procedures in an electronic environment.

Redaction is the separation of disclosable from non-disclosable information by blocking out individual words, sentences or paragraphs or the removal of whole pages or sections prior to the release of the document. In the paper environment some organizations will know redaction as extracts when whole pages are removed, or deletions where only a section of text is affected.

Principles of redaction

1 Redaction should always be reversible – it should never result in permanent removal of text. It should always be carried out on copies, whether paper or electronic.
2 Redaction is carried out in order to edit exempt details from a document. It should be used when one or two individual words, a sentence or paragraph, a name, address or signature needs to be removed.
3 If so much information has to be withheld that a document becomes nonsensical, the entire document should be withheld. In the case of paper documents the same principle should apply to individual pages.
4 When undertaking redaction, reviewers and assessors should consider whether any other factors are important for the understanding of the material. For example, if colour makes meaning clear in a paper document, a redacted colour copy should be released.
5 Redaction should be performed or overseen by staff that are knowledgeable about the records and can determine what material is exempt. If those staff

identifying such material do not carry out redaction themselves, their instructions must be specific, e.g. 'Memo dated . . ., paragraph no . . ., line starting . . . and ending . . .' etc. The consequences for misunderstanding unclear instructions hardly need mentioning.

6 Under Freedom of Information, applicants may request that information be presented to them in electronic form. For paper documents, this will usually mean scanning the redacted version of the material. If, however, the level of resources required to do the scanning would make this unduly onerous, the Freedom of Information Act (section 11) allows the organization to set aside the applicant's stated preference on the grounds of practicability. The Act also permits that a summary of the document be transcribed. If a large percentage of the document needs to be redacted, this option of summarizing its contents may be worth considering as a more viable alternative to redaction.

Identifying material for redaction

All organizations should have staff able to identify information that may be exempt under the Freedom of Information Act. Ideally they should have a good knowledge of the records being reviewed for release. Often this is not a problem, since it is usually the case that the people making the exemption decision are from that part of the organization either responsible for the function in question or for creating the records in the first place.

In order to conform fully with requests for information, it is essential that only exempt material be redacted. A whole sentence or paragraph should not be removed if only one or two words are non-disclosable, unless release would place the missing words in context and make their content or meaning clear.

Reviewers and assessors should also consider that earlier statements in a document might suggest the content of removed material. For example, if a paragraph refers to reports from overt sources, and the following paragraph refers to reports from covert sources, as well as removing the words 'covert sources', 'overt sources' would also need to be removed or the meaning of the missing words from the second paragraph could be inferred.

Records also need to be checked for other copies of the same documents so that redaction is carried out consistently, and indexes have to be checked to ensure that they do not contain details of the redacted material.

Keeping records of redaction work

Once redactions have been identified and agreed with any other interested parties, decisions need to be recorded. The majority of Freedom of Information Acts contain provision for appeals against the non-disclosure of information. Authorities, therefore, need to be in a position to reply effectively to any appeals. For some organizations, simply keeping a copy of the released copy of a document has been enough, with a note explaining the reasons for redaction. For others an electronic tracking system has proved effective. If multiple requests are made for the same information, this will show what decisions have been made in prior requests.

If more detailed records of decisions are required, this has usually been done on a standard form recording as much of the following information as is relevant:

1 *An identifying reference, registered file number, case file number or electronic document reference*. This identifier can be anything that suits the organization concerned, but must enable easy identification and retrieval of the document. The format chosen should be used consistently.
2 *Precise details of the material removed* (this need not describe the content, but should show which section of the document has been withheld, e.g. paragraph 2 of page 4. However, if only one or two words are being withheld, these details will need to be exact to enable precise identification). This might be achieved by keeping a copy of the original document, with the details to be redacted highlighted, as well as the redacted version.
3 *The reason for non-disclosure of the information*. If one or more Freedom of Information exemptions apply, these should all be noted, along with the particular reasons that apply in each case.
4 Any *comments* made by reviewers and other organizations or individuals consulted.

Methods of redaction
Paper records

1 *Cover-up tape* – The simplest form of redaction is to use a high quality cover-up tape that can be placed on the original documents over the areas to be redacted, taking care that no parts of words are showing. By making a photocopy of the redacted text, an access version is produced ready for presentation. The tape is white, and acts in much the same way as if using correction fluid, but can be reused several times. Care needs to be taken where original documents are not in very good condition. There may be a danger that writing is lifted off the document when the cover-up tape is removed.
2 *Blacking/whiting out* – Another simple solution is to photocopy the original document and use a black marker pen to block out the sensitive material. The redacted version should then be photocopied again to produce an access version. The further photocopy is necessary as information redacted using marker pen can be read when held up to light. The same process can be employed substituting a good-quality correction fluid or marker pen. Redacted text must not be visible before making the second photocopy, which again is necessary as correction fluid can be easily removed.
3 *Scalpel* – A seemingly drastic but perhaps the most precise and secure method

of redaction is to use a scalpel, where the exempt material is physically removed from a photocopy, leaving no risk of text being visible in the released version. The material to be redacted is then cut from the photocopy using an artist's scalpel or similar tool, leaving a 'doily', which is then photocopied again to provide the redacted document.

4 *Photocopier with redaction facilities* – Photocopiers are available which, in addition to normal copying functions, also have facilities to automatically remove marked-out areas on a document. They provide a secure method of redaction, as there is no possibility of the removed text being visible after copying. However, they are limited in their effectiveness as the programmes can, at present, only remove paragraphs and stand-alone areas of text such as addresses or signatures. They cannot reliably detect small areas of data such as sentences or individual words. A photocopier of this nature would probably be cost-effective only for organizations carrying out a large volume of redaction, where savings on more conventional materials would outweigh the cost of investing in such a copier.

Electronic records

The redaction of digital records is a relatively new area of records management practice, and raises unique issues and potential risks. The simplest type of electronic record to redact is a plain text file, in which there is a one-to-one correspondence between bytes and displayable characters. Because of this direct correspondence, redacting these formats is simply a matter of deleting the displayed information – once the file is saved, the deleted information cannot be recovered. However, the majority of electronic records created using office systems, such as Microsoft Office, are stored in proprietary, binary-encoded formats. Binary formats do not have this simple and direct correlation, and may contain significant information which is not displayed to the user, and the presence of which may therefore not be apparent. They may incorporate change histories, audit trails, or embedded metadata, by means of which deleted information can be recovered or simple redaction processes otherwise circumvented. These formats are also usually the property of the software house that developed them, and these companies have 'typically' regarded providing public documentation of these formats as against their commercial interests. Consequently, the mechanisms by which information is stored within these formats are often poorly understood. In addition, cryptographic and semantic analysis techniques can be used to identify redacted information. It is therefore essential that any redaction technique be secured to eliminate the possibility of redacted information being recovered.

The redaction of electronic records should always be carried out in accordance with the following principles:

1 The original or master version of an electronic record must never be redacted

– redaction must always be carried out on a new copy of the record, either in paper or electronic format.

2 Redaction must irreversibly remove the required information from the redacted copy of the record. The information must be completely removed from the bit stream, not simply from the displayable record.

3 Redaction should always be carried out using methods which have been fully security tested.

4 Electronic redaction should be carried out in a controlled and secure environment that provides access only to those trained and authorized to carry out redaction.

5 All intermediary stages of the redaction process should be deleted. Only the original record and the appropriately redacted copy should be retained.

There are a number of different approaches to electronic redaction:

1 *Traditional redaction* – For electronic records, which can be printed as a hard copy, traditional redaction techniques, as described above, can be applied. Either the record may be printed and redaction carried out on the printed copy, or the information may be redacted from an electronic copy, which is then printed. If the redacted copy is required in electronic format, this can be created by scanning the redacted paper copy into an appropriate format, such as Adobe Portable Document Format (PDF).

2 *Format redaction* – Records may be redacted electronically in their original format. This may be carried out either using deletion tools within the creating software, or by using specialized redaction software. This approach must be treated with extreme caution, because of the possibility that deleted information may still be recoverable, and the potential for information to remain hidden within non-displayable portions of the bit stream.

3 *Conversion* – An electronic record may be redacted through a combination of information deletion and conversion to a different format. Certain formats, such as plain ASCII text files, contain displayable information only. Conversion to this format will therefore eliminate any information that may be hidden in non-displayable portions of a bit stream.

4 *Round trip redaction* – The redacted record may be required to be made available in its original format – for example, to preserve complex formatting. In such cases, an extension of the conversion approach may be applicable. Round tripping entails the conversion of the record to another format, followed by conversion back to the original format in such a way that the conversion process removes all evidence of the redacted information. Information deletion may be carried out either prior to conversion, or in the intermediary format. This approach requires a thorough understanding of the formats and conversion processes involved, and the mechanisms by which information is transferred during conversion.

There are several software packages now available which will redact electronic records effectively. Some can also be linked to a scanner to enable the redaction of paper records to be undertaken electronically.

Usability

The electronic records management system must maximize the usability of the system for the end user. This is the main, if not the only, way that user buy-in can be maintained. User buy-in is essential if the organization is going to create an effective corporate system.

At the heart of usability is the file plan. Indeed almost the whole of the efficacy of an electronic records management system depends on the file plan. The subject has been examined in detail in Chapter 6 but, from a usability point of view, it is worth repeating some of the significant features:

1 Make the file plan simple – aim for a maximum of three levels, although there may be some functional areas that justify more.
2 Have a naming convention scheme, so that everybody in the organization can retrieve information they need with minimum difficulty.
3 Think corporately when thinking of usability. The electronic records management system, almost by definition, is a corporate system and everybody in the organization, as far as possible, needs to buy in to it.
4 Promote flexibility in the file plan. You want everyone in the organization to use the system so consider how their ways of working might be incorporated. For example, arrange for a system of stored favourites or aliases in handy/personal folders.
5 Ensure that everyone is aware of the benefits of the file plan (and the electronic records management system generally) – for example, that corporate information is available to all who need it, not just to those who have created it.

In the context of access, consider how far you will allow the user to allocate access metadata. For example, how far will you permit the creation of new folders (see the section on roles above)? Will there be any checking of the allocation of titles to folders and/or to documents? Who in the business areas will be authorized to allocate or advise on protective markings? Answers to all these questions depend very much on the ways of working or even on the culture of particular organizations but they will have a significant impact on the usability of the electronic records management system.

Another key element of usability is the provision of an appropriate viewer or browser, which should be simple and easy to use and one with which users are either familiar or on which they can easily be trained. But even this can lead to other questions for consideration. For example, quick and easy retrieval of information can be promoted by continued management of access demand and of appropriate access permissions. The pattern of demand can lead to modifications to the access control system that may make retrieval even simpler and quicker. Also, effective presentation of the information once it has been retrieved can help the user to interpret or use the record effectively. This might also extend to a need to view metadata, especially in situations where one organization has inherited the records of another.

Security

Information and information systems are valuable assets to an organization, playing a major role in supporting strategic objectives, implementing policies and procedures, and undertaking specific activities. The security of this information is therefore vital to any organization's reputation and success. Information security is achieved by applying best practice measures and controls. Many of these controls are technical and will be the speciality of ICT staff but many are also applicable to everyone in the organization. The latter should be incorporated into an Information Security Policy or Manual and everyone in the organization must have a responsibility for ensuring that information is managed properly and suitably protected. The following pages give a broad outline of what such a manual might include.

Standards

The most significant standard on information security is ISO 17799 – *Information technology, Security techniques, Code of practice for information security management*. It provides best-practice recommendations on information security management, which is defined as 'the preservation of confidentiality (ensuring that information is accessible only to those authorized to have access), integrity (safeguarding the accuracy and completeness of information and processing methods) and availability (ensuring that authorized users have access to information and associated assets when required)'. The recommendations include risk assessments, security policy, asset management, physical and environmental security, access control and business continuity management.

Complementary to this standard is ISO 27001 – *Information Security Management – Specification with Guidance for Use*, which describes the basis for an assessment of an organization's information security management system; this was formerly part 2 of the British Standard BS 7799. It is intended to provide the foundation for third-party audit, and is harmonized with other management standards, such as ISO 9001 and ISO 14001. The basic objective of the standard is to help establish and maintain an effective information management system, using a continual improvement approach. It implements OECD (Organization for Economic Co-operation and Development) principles, governing security of information and network systems. The standard is arranged into eleven areas:

- Security policy
- Organization
- Asset management
- Human resources
- Physical and environment
- Communications and operations management
- Access control
- System development and maintenance
- Security incident management
- Business continuity management
- Compliance and audit.

The Information Security Forum (ISF) has produced the *Standard of Good Practice for Information Security*. It addresses information security from a business perspective and provides a practical and business-focused statement of good practice. It is available from the ISF website at www.isfsecuritystandard.com/home.htm.

The Information Systems Audit and Control Association (ISACA) is a global organization for information governance, control, security and audit professionals. It has developed a standard for information security entitled *Control Objectives for Information and Related Technology* (COBIT). It is a set of best practices for information management to assist managers, auditors and IT users in maximizing the benefits derived through the use of information technology.

Legislation

There are several acts and regulations that impinge on the holding and processing of information. These include:

1 *Data Protection Act 1998* – requires anyone who handles personal information to comply with a number of important principles. It also gives individuals rights over their personal information.
2 *Freedom of Information Act 2000* – intended to promote a culture of openness and accountability amongst public authorities in the UK by providing people with rights of access to the information held by them.
3 *Human Rights Act 1998* – incorporates rights and freedoms guaranteed by the European Convention on Human Rights, including freedom of expression, freedom of thought, conscience and religion.
4 *Copyright, Designs and Patents Act 1988* – gives the creators of certain kinds of material rights to control ways their material can be used. These rights start as soon as the material is recorded in writing or in any other way. They cover copying, adapting, distributing, communicating to the public by electronic transmission (including by broadcasting and in an on demand service), renting

or lending copies to the public and performing in public. In many cases, the author will also have the right to be identified on their works and to object if their work is distorted or mutilated.

5 *Computer Misuse Act 1990* – under which hacking of computers and the introduction of viruses are criminal offences.

6 *Regulation of Investigatory Powers Act 2000* – permits the interception and monitoring of e-communications in order to ensure regulatory compliance and detect crime or other unauthorized use.

7 *Electronic Communications Act 2000* – makes provision to facilitate the use of electronic communications and electronic data storage.

Aims and benefits

Information security management enables the sharing of information in a manner that ensures the appropriate protection of that information. It should aim to protect information in order to:

- safeguard the accuracy and completeness of information and information systems
- minimize damage in the event of a security breach
- ensure that authorized users have access to information as and when required
- ensure that information is accessible only to those authorized
- ensure business continuity
- give everyone confidence in the availability and integrity of an organization's information and electronic records management systems.

Responsibilities

It is the responsibility of everyone in the organization to ensure that information management facilities and services are used appropriately and that information security policies and procedures are properly adhered to. This will include:

- using up-to-date anti-virus software
- not removing ICT equipment from the organization's premises without authorization
- not installing unauthorized software on the organization's systems and not changing any hardware components
- abiding by health and safety considerations relating to the use of computer equipment
- reporting information security incidents or problems to the appropriate point (usually an IT helpdesk)
- adopting good practice in respect of passwords (for example, not sharing passwords, protecting password and user identity)

- not responding to phishing messages
- locking workstations when not being used
- not leaving disks, CDs and other portable hardware on unattended desks.

Risk assessments

Any information security policy must be supplemented by a risk assessment procedure. Such an assessment (and regular risk analyses) forms the foundation of the policy itself. The process of risk assessment has three elements:

1 *Identification* – regularly checking and identifying potential threats to systems, including unauthorized access, heating and ventilation, etc.
2 *Estimation* – However many risks to an organization, the effects are likely to be few, usually the loss of critical systems, site or personnel and the denial of access to systems or premises. The risks to electronic records, of course, may be significant and it is essential that there is a back-up system (standard in most ICT infrastructures).
3 *Evaluation* – An indicator system should be used to evaluate the risks, as shown in Table 9.1.

Table 9.1 Risk indication system

Impact		Likelihood	
1	major problem; mixture of business risks and project risks	a b	high – likely to happen medium to high – could happen
2	could cause problems – mainly project risks	c	medium – might happen in right conditions
3	unlikely to cause real problems	d	low to medium – probably will not happen
		e	low – very unlikely

Information security is a constantly evolving subject because of the ever-increasing scale and complexity of threats, brought about by continuous improvements in technology and unstable political situations. It is always useful to keep abreast of developments by subscribing to discussion forums or newsletters.

APPENDIX
Sample table of requirements for access

Ref	Requirement	M/HD/D*	Comments
4.1	The system must provide an authentication mechanism which controls access to the electronic records management system (such as an individual user identification/password log in	M	
4.2	The system must support the use of user roles that will be used in controlling access to the system and its functions	M	
4.3	The system must support the use of protective markings for groups, teams and individuals	M	
4.4	The system should support a hierarchy of protective marking categories as follows: • Unrestricted • Restricted • Confidential • Secret	D	
4.5	The system must allow user access to folders, sub-folders and documents in line with the user role or protective marking group to which they belong	M	
4.6	The system must ensure that users cannot access folders, sub-folders or records to which they do not have the appropriate access rights	M	
4.7	The system should allow users to locate metadata for records that they are not allowed to view	HD	
4.8	The system should record whether information is released under the Freedom of Information Act 2000 or Data Protection Act 1998	HD	
4.9	The system must allow for amendment of access control rights for each user by a systems administrator at any time	M	
4.10	The system must restrict the ability to define and maintain available access control markings to a systems administrator	M	
4.11	The system should ensure that a sub-folder inherits the access control markings allocated to its parent folder	HD	
4.12	The system must be capable of automatically upgrading the security category of a folder to the level of the highest rating of its contents	M	
4.13	The system should notify the records manager prior to the termination of an access control marking	HD	

* M – mandatory; HD – highly desirable; D – desirable

Part 3

Implementation

10

Main issues for implementation

Designing the electronic records management system involves a great deal of technical planning and discussion. Implementation is a much more practical challenge. It will involve a great many management skills – project management, procurement, change management and training. All these are examined in the following chapters. This chapter looks at some general points relating to implementation, at particular issues that may affect it, such as hybrid records, e-mail and vital records, and at procedures for a post-implementation review.

The key aspect of the implementation of electronic records management, and its main objective, is to integrate the new system with current policies and practices so that as soon as possible it becomes the norm. This is quite a challenge. As the following chapters try to explain, it is not something that will happen overnight and it requires dedication and understanding by all parties concerned. The risks involved can be minimized through careful planning and documentation of the implementation process. In order to plan effectively, you will need to take into consideration several factors, such as organizational culture, current IT infrastructure, financial and other constraints, and overall business strategies. Implementation will vary from organization to organization but there will be several common activities:

- communication – keeping staff informed of progress, how the implementation affects them and where they can get advice
- making available policies and procedures relating to electronic records management
- evaluating available skills and organizing training events
- organizing support functions such as accommodation
- assigning and reviewing access rights to records
- issuing formal reports for management and project board members
- gathering information relating to implementation – take-up, user problems, change control, etc.

An underlying requirement, which has to be borne in mind at all times during implementation, is that information must always be readily available. The business of the organization cannot stop while machines are being configured, data is being converted, etc. This can, of course, be achieved technically but also needs to be planned carefully so that all users are confident that their working routines will not be unduly disrupted.

You may be interested in the following list whose contents have been garnered from a trawl of several websites on electronic records management projects. It describes some of the lessons learnt by organizations, particularly in the implementation phase:

- identify key partners for the project
- design role-specific training for project team members
- develop fully funded modules including a phased roll-out of the system
- test for user acceptance throughout the project
- integrate electronic records management with other systems
- considerable effort may be required to develop detailed internal procedures
- senior management buy-in is vital (but, with enough determination and resolution, a system can be implemented without it)
- the culture change involved must receive attention at all times
- focus on the users' ability to access the information they need to do their jobs rather than emphasizing the ideal system that is to be created
- installation of the ERM system is always a much bigger task than anyone thinks.

Hybrid records

Definition

A hybrid record is one that comprises both electronic and physical documents and which relates to the same function, activity or task in an organization.

Management principles

The difficulties concerned with the management of hybrid records have tended to be exaggerated. When these difficulties are analysed, they come down to one principal objective: information (not records) on the same or similar business function should be linked. So, when you interrogate an electronic records management system, you need to know whether there are any related paper records (or, for that matter, any records in any other format). In order to facilitate this functionality, the system must be able to capture and maintain metadata relating to physical records. This requires the creation of markers – metadata profiles of records that are held outside the electronic records management system. The markers must be allocated to folders in the same way as electronic documents. They should contain metadata that will enable the system to locate and manage physical (usually paper) records and to allocate management controls to them. These controls will include access, security, disposal and retrieval.

Figure 10.1 shows a hybrid folder containing both electronic records and markers representing physical records.

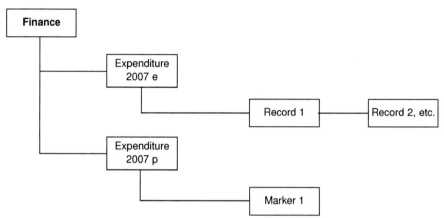

Figure 10.1 Hybrid folder management
The hybrid folder 'Expenditure 2007' has an electronic element (shown by the folder 'Expenditure 2007 e' containing records 1 and 2, etc.) and a physical element shown by the folder 'Expenditure 2007 p' (which holds metadata about physical records for the main folder) and the marker 'Marker 1' (which holds the metadata for the physical record).

Also in this context it should be said that, when it comes to the appraisal of hybrid records for medium- to long-term retention, perhaps even for archival preservation, the paper and electronic records must be dealt with at the same time. Most appraisal, selection and transfer of paper records takes place about 20 to 25 years after their creation but, if there are any that relate to more recent electronic records, and they are selected with them, they should be transferred to the archive at the same time. Furthermore, they should be allocated to the same archival classification series if that means maintaining the provenance of the records.

Requirements

At the end of the chapter is a sample table of requirements for hybrid records in an electronic records management system.

E-mail

E-mail has become increasingly important in recent years. Not only is it a communications tool, it is now used to record important corporate decisions. It has been estimated that up to 80% of such decisions are now communicated in this way. If organizations are to maintain a comprehensive corporate record of their business activities, arrangements must be made for e-mails to be captured into the corporate electronic records management system. They will, in most cases, need to be linked with complementary records in the form of correspondence, reports and other forms. E-mail systems, therefore, need to be integrated with electronic records management systems; most generic systems handle e-mail effectively and thus achieve this objective.

Managing e-mail as corporate records would normally involve a user identifying whether the e-mail is a corporate record in the first place and then capturing it into the ERM system. This will then associate it with other records by placing it in the appropriate folder or sub-folder, allocate the metadata and ensure that it is disposed of when it is no longer required (in accordance with the appropriate disposal schedule).

E-mails that are not considered to be corporate records can be left in the e-mail management system where (by common practice) they will be deleted after three months.

Vital records

An important part of the conversion to electronic records management is the identification of vital records. In the electronic environment some of these may be in the same configuration as in the paper environment but checks should be made to ensure that the organization's vital information (as opposed to mere records) is being correctly identified as the change takes place.

Vital records are those without which an organization could not continue to operate. They are the records which contain information needed to re-establish the business of the organization in the event of a disaster and which protect the assets and interests of the organization. It is estimated that up to 10% of an organization's records can be classified as vital. A distinction may be drawn between vital records and emergency records:

- *vital records*: those whose long-term preservation must be ensured to allow the organization's functions to continue
- *emergency records*: those which are required for immediate access but which are not crucial in the long term.

The following guidance covers both these types.

Identification

The records manager needs to analyse the business and the records it produces in order to:

- identify critical processes and functions

- identify the key internal and external dependencies on which these processes rely
- identify external influences which may have an impact on critical processes and functions
- identify the records relating to the critical processes and functions.

Since it is expensive to make special protection arrangements for records it is important not to be tempted to include everything that *might* be vital. Key points to consider are:

- whether the processes or functions can be re-established without the records concerned
- the senior management view of the importance of the functions to which the records relate
- the length of time for which information is required.

For the purpose of identifying vital records, all records might be classified as follows:

- *vital* – those records without which your organization cannot continue to operate and which cannot easily be reproduced, if at all, from other sources
- *important* – can be reproduced from original sources but only at considerable expense
- *useful* – loss would cause temporary inconvenience
- *non-essential* – no value beyond immediate purpose.

Table 10.1 (on the next page) has some examples of these four categories.

When vital electronic records (as well as paper records) have been identified, they should be documented so that everyone in the organization is aware of them. Such documentation should include:

- *Description* – category or type of vital record
- *Disposal reference* – cross-reference to any disposal schedule pertaining to the record(s)
- *Format* – how the vital record is protected
- *Location* – where protected vital record is held (the back-up copy)
- *Supporting documents* – description of any supporting documents such as finding aids.

As we have seen from the examination of preservation, the storage of records in electronic form may involve significant risks, such as technical obsolescence, but many of these can be avoided by the use of adequate storage plans and strategies.

Table 10.1   Categories of importance of records

Category	Examples
1. Vital records	Legal documents, including current contracts
	Corporate plans
	Manuals of instruction
	Minutes of management board meetings
	Current accounts (payable and receivable)
	Records identified for legal retention and other records required for evidential/legal purposes
	Computer software programmes and data
	Indexes and other finding aids to records
	Systems administration documentation
2. Important records	Minutes of meetings of named committees and sub-committees
	Training manuals
	Directories
	File plans
3. Useful records	Correspondence files
	Presentations for regular undertakings (conferences, training courses, etc.)
	Training modules
	Management reports
4. Non-essential records	Visitors' records
	Information about specific events (which have taken place)
	Advertisements (e.g. recruitment)
	Newsletters

Post-implementation review

By the time implementation of the electronic records management system is complete, your organization will have been involved in a considerable investment of resources – money, staff, time and, perhaps most important, goodwill. Now is the time to demonstrate to senior management and other stakeholders that the project has been completed successfully, efficiently and effectively. In addition, you will need to demonstrate that the expected benefits of introducing the new system have been realized. All these are part of the post-implementation review.

Who is going to undertake the review and what will it cover?

The review should be led by an independent person – independent, that is, from anyone who was part of the project board or project team. The records manager will almost certainly need to be available to provide guidance and advice, but the review itself must be seen to be unbiased.

The scope of the review will depend on the nature and extent of the project but, if you have delivered a new system to the whole organization, it is, of course, likely to be extensive. You should, for example, gather views from as wide a spectrum of business areas as possible. Also, the culture of your organization might influence the character and perhaps the timing of the review. A large organization might want to hire consultants to undertake the review; a smaller set-up may settle for a peer review and a short report to senior management. Whatever the size of the organization, a review taken between six and twelve months after completion of the implementation is common.

Generally the review will cover the following areas:

- *Appropriateness* – does the current need for an electronic records management system correspond to the original need, or has technology moved on so much that it has overtaken the project? Is the new system appropriate to the organization's business needs?
- *Efficiency* – is implementation of the electronic records management system showing a reduction of overall costs for records and information management? Does the implementation compare favourably with similar undertakings in other organizations?
- *Effectiveness* – Have all the objectives been achieved (bearing in mind how much resource was available)? Do outcomes compare favourably with needs? Is the organization meeting all relevant standards in the management of its records and information? Has the organization realized all the benefits that it set out (see page 42 for details about measuring benefits)?

Conclusion

Remember that you are not alone when it comes to planning and implementing electronic records management systems. In some sectors some good communities of practice have been established. These have proved useful and supportive by:

- sharing information, knowledge and ideas with colleagues across the sector
- helping each other
- changing the way similar organizations work (for example, central government departments) so that good practice becomes common practice.

Responses to the implementation of electronic records management systems have varied in recent years, from acceptance to indifference to passive resistance right up to active resistance. After a year or two, however, you will find that, while staff may feel nostalgic towards their old paper systems, few of them will want to go back to it.

APPENDIX

Sample table of requirements for hybrid records

Ref	Requirement	M/HD/D*	Comments
5.1	The system must be able to support the management of physical/paper records and folders in a manner that is closely integrated with the management of electronic records and folders	M	
5.2	The system must be able to define physical/paper folders in the file plan	M	
5.3	The system must be able to define hybrid folders in the file plan	M	
5.4	The system must be able to support the use of metadata for physical/paper folders and hybrid folders	M	
5.5	The system must be able to define a different metadata set for physical/paper folders than that for electronic folders (so that, for example, the physical location of the former can be recorded)	M	
5.6	The system must enable the creation of markers – metadata profiles of physical/paper records which are held outside the system	M	
5.7	The system should allow markers to denote different types of physical record, for example volume, map, plan, video	HD	
5.8	The system must be able to search for and retrieve markers and physical folders, and electronic records and folders, by a single integrated search	M	
5.9	The system must be able to control user access to metadata about markers and physical/paper folders consistent with the controls for electronic records and folders	M	
5.10	The system must be able to support the allocation of a disposal schedule to a physical/paper folder	M	
*M – mandatory; HD – highly desirable; D – desirable			

11

Project management

This chapter suggests a broad project management methodology for implementing electronic records management and gives references to the wealth of advice that is available on the subject.

In Chapter 3 we saw how project management needs to feature in the business case for electronic records management. This chapter examines the subject in a little more detail and in the context of implementing a new system.

Introduction

More and more work is undertaken by specific projects as opposed to being part of mainstream operations and activities in an organization. The main driver for this has been economic, but the increased concentration has also been seen to deliver better products in a timely fashion. Since the 1950s project management has emerged as a specific discipline for organizing and managing resources in such a way that they deliver all the work required to complete a project within defined scope, quality, time and cost constraints.

Most of project management is common sense. What the various methodologies do is to offer a structured approach that will enable you to get the job done more effectively and efficiently.

One basic decision to make when embarking on a large project is whether you are going to use in-house expertise or employ specialist consultants. In implementing electronic records management it is very likely that you will want to use outside technical experts. Management of the project, however, should always be controlled internally. If you decide to use a substantial amount of your own organization's resources, it may be necessary to organize some training for staff. This will almost certainly be time and money well invested. Such is the ubiquity of project management that there will be a long-term benefit for the organization and its staff.

Sample project for implementing electronic records management

This suggestion is based largely on a methodology commonly used in the public sector in the UK and widely recognized in the UK private sector – PRINCE 2 (**PR**ojects **IN** Controlled Environments), which was first established in 1989. The key features of the methodology are:

- Its focus on business justification
- A defined organization structure for the project management team
- Its product-based planning approach
- Its emphasis on dividing the project into manageable and controllable stages
- Its flexibility to be applied at a level appropriate to the project.

For more information on this particular methodology see www.ogc.gov.uk/methods_ prince_2.asp.

Main processes

The main processes that you will need to go through with an electronic records management project are illustrated in Figure 11.1.

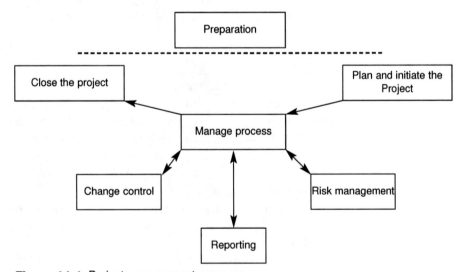

Figure 11.1 Project management processes

Preparation

You should sit down and think about the project and its components before you actually start planning it. These are the main issues to take into account:

1   *Business case* – remind yourself of the business case so that the project proceeds in accordance with its plans and promises. These will include the aims and objectives of the project, and its overall vision.

2   *Roles and responsibilities* – who are going to fill the positions of the project board and project team? You will need to appoint to the following:

3   *Project Board*

    — *Senior Responsible Owner* – this is the person, usually a very senior member of staff, who has overall strategic responsibility for records and information management in the organization. Often known as the Project Sponsor, they will champion the project and ensure that it is actively reviewed throughout its life. They are likely to be the person who will need to deal with delicate negotiations on funding and other resources with finance directors and chief executives. A major area of responsibility is to be accountable for the delivery of planned benefits. This person will also chair the project board meetings.

    — *Project Manager* – the person responsible for ensuring that the project is delivered on time, to budget and to the required quality standard. They will manage relationships with various groups of people and individuals involved with the project and will ensure that it is resourced effectively (including the use of consultants). They will provide regular reports to the project board and project team. For an electronic records management project this person is likely to be the records manager.

    — *Team Leaders* – Each business area affected by the project should have a representative. There needs to be some limit on these, of course, in order not to make the size of the board unwieldy. The objective is to have about three or four people who will speak for the organization's business requirements of electronic records management. For example, if it has a public-facing function, you will need someone from that part of the organization. You will almost certainly need someone from the ICT area.

    — *HR/Training* – there should be specific representation from the human resources part of the organization, someone who has a particular responsibility for training. This will be a major part of the project and will need to be scheduled into existing training and awareness programmes.

    — *External* – you may need more than one representative for outside interests. If you are contracting out some of the work of implementation, then the outside company must be represented. Generally there would be one main contractor who may or may not (depending on contract terms) sub-contract to other companies. Representation from that main contractor will usually be sufficient for the project board. There may also be representation from external stakeholders if, for example, your organization has business dealings with government departments or with a group of companies.

4   *Project Team*
    — *Project Manager* – the project manager will normally head the project team and chair its meetings.
    — *Team Leaders* – these will be representatives of the business areas that will need to undertake activities to complete the project. Each will have a specific role definition and a plan of actions that need to be taken. For example, in a public authority you will need a Freedom of Information representative to ensure that procedures (such as redaction) meet FOI requirements; you may need someone from the facilities management side of the organization who will need to take action on services and accommodation.
    — *Communication* – this can be a vital role in the team. An undertaking such as this will mean very significant change for the organization and there should be someone in the team with responsibility for communicating progress, requirements and action to all parts of the organization. This will mean making use of intranets, meetings, newsletters and marketing events. We have already seen how important it is to obtain user buy-in for an electronic records management system and in this respect the project communications co-ordinator has a vital role to play.
    — *Project Administrator* – a project of this size will very likely need someone to maintain the project plan, handle the support functions like tracking, reporting and meetings, and manage issue and risk logs. In general they will provide administrative support to the project manager.
5   *Stakeholders* – it is important to identify the organization's stakeholders. Most, if not all, are likely to be affected by an electronic records management project. You will need to decide how the stakeholders are going to be involved or perhaps formally represented on the project. You will need to make this decision mainly on a judgement of how influential they might be in the success of the project. They may, for example, have a strategic influence (such as a member of the management board) or they may be in a position to exercise managerial control over parts of the electronic records management system. The major stakeholders, of course, are the users – those on whom you are going to rely on to operate the new system. How are you going to involve them in the project? You will need to strike a balance between taking in the full range of their views (perhaps by holding focus groups and consultation meetings) and merely keeping them informed of progress. This will depend very much on the nature and culture of your organization but the important thing is to involve them in some way.
6   *Planning* – how are you going to document the project plan? PRINCE 2 has well tried methods for doing this, which you will probably adopt at the planning stage. At the initial thinking stage, however, you may wish to draw up a route map, giving a broad outline of the path the project will take. This can be a useful device for involving stakeholders and other interested parties

at an early stage. It lets them know immediately what the project is about and gives them an indication of how they might be affected. The route map can be as simple or as complicated as you wish, but it must be able to be appreciated and understood by everyone in the organization who is likely to be affected by the project. A suggested map is shown at the end of this chapter.

7 *Roll out* – consider how you are going to introduce the new electronic records management system. This decision is likely to depend on the size of the organization.

— Will you introduce a pilot system in one part of the organization first? If so, will this generate conflict between the chosen and the by-passed? How would a pilot in any particular part of the organization affect business process, such as dealings with outside customers or contractors? In what part of the organization will a pilot have the most effect in terms of lessons learnt, opportunities for other members of staff to see the outcomes, and ability to rectify any problems?

— Once you are entirely satisfied that the new system is ready, will you roll it out gradually or will you adopt what has come to be called the 'big bang' approach – introduce it to the whole organization at the same time?

— When the new system is rolled out, will you run the old system (whether it is paper-based or a local area network) in parallel for a set time? This is a fine judgement in many cases and also dependent on the culture of the organization. Experience shows that most organizations in this position have grasped the nettle, put confidence in the testing of the new system and dropped the old system on implementation day.

8 *Interface with other systems* – consider what effect a new electronic records management system will have on existing systems and strategies, including the IT strategy, intranets and websites, e-mail and any databases (such as those in financial and human resources areas, which are quite common). Some preliminary discussions with key personnel in those areas may help to eliminate any difficulty that might have been encountered in planning the project.

9 *Documentation* – the PRINCE 2 methodology recommends particular documentation. You may want to either streamline this or use other documentation with which your organization is more familiar. Where and how will the project documentation be kept, and how far will it be made available to others in the organization? Is the documentation covered by disposal schedules?

10 *Reviews* – you may wish to commission independent reviews of the project at key stages. The methodology incorporates internal reviews but, if resources are available, it can often be beneficial to employ the services of an outside consultant to give an unbiased view of project progress. In UK Government circles this is known as a Gateway Review and follows a structured auditing and reporting path. It is an effective way of identifying risks to projects and ensuring that a project is delivered on time and to budget.

Plan and initiate

Planning and initiating the project will revolve round two main documents – the requirements catalogue and the project initiation document.

The *requirements catalogue* should describe in detail precisely what is required of the electronic records management system. It will be divided into those functional areas that have been described in Part 2 above (file plan, appraisal, preservation and access). A great deal of work has been undertaken in recent years to draw up generic functional requirements for electronic records management systems. There are two main sources that you can draw upon as a basis for compiling your organization's specific requirements:

MoReq2 are *Model **Requirements** for the management of electronic records* – the result of a project undertaken by the DLM Forum, a body set up in 1994 for the promotion of greater co-operation in the field of archives. See www.cornwell.co.uk/ edrm/moreq.asp.

The UK National Archives has published *Requirements for Electronic Records Management Systems*, which comprises four parts:

1 Functional requirements
2 Metadata standard
3 Reference document
4 Implementation guide.

See www.nationalarchives.gov.uk/electronicrecords/reqs2002/default.htm. An example of a catalogue entry is given in Figure 11.2.

It will also be useful if the requirements catalogue includes a glossary and/or definitions of abbreviations.

The *project initiation document* (PID) should contain all those undertakings you might naturally associate with planning. Since the PRINCE 2 methodology is principally concerned with products, the PID will identify and analyse those products or deliverables that the project requires. It should identify the activities required to create the products so that the effort needed for each can be estimated and scheduled into the progress plan. Typically the PID will cover the following:

1 Document history – drafts and revisions to the PID.
2 Purpose of the document – a typical entry would be 'To define the project to form the basis of its management and assessment of its success'.
3 Background of the project – why it has been set up, its context and drivers, and how it has reached this stage.
4 Definition of the project, which will include:
   — Objectives
   — Methodology
   — Scope

Requirement	1	Transfer system – remote delivery	
Priority	Mandatory	Owner	Project Team
Functional requirement			
The transfer system user interface provided to regional business areas should be browser based and independent of any requirement to install software on the business area's desktop or network.			
Benefits			
Allows for the deployment to business areas with locked-down desktops or thin client solutions.			
Suggested solutions			
Comments			
This should not exclude the use of standard commercial plug-ins that could be expected to be available on a standard PC, for example a PDF reader. Certain functions of transfer may require functionality that cannot be provided through a browser.			
Resolution			
Related requirements			
3 – Transfer documentation 4 – Physical transfer			

— Deliverables

Figure 11.2 Example of a catalogue entry
Reproduced with kind permission from The National Archives

- — Exclusions
- — Constraints
- — Interfaces
- — Assumptions.
5 Organization of the project – board and team structure, roles and responsibilities and reporting procedures.
6 Communication plan.
7 Quality plan – how the quality of the deliverables will be measured.
8 Tolerances – generally phrased as, for example, '+/- 5% of budget; +/- 5% of days for deliverables'.
9 Controls – you may want to breakdown the project into stages (as the PRINCE 2 methodology suggests) and make stage reports as part of the control procedures. Other means of control are the production of monthly highlight reports, regular meetings and one-to-one discussions with the Chief Executive or management board representative.
10 Stakeholder analysis – a description of all stakeholders, their interest in the project and how they will be involved.

Managing progress

Key documents in managing the project are the monitoring plan, issues log and risk log.

The *monitoring plan* used in many PRINCE 2 undertakings comprises a Gantt chart. Gantt Charts are extremely useful project management tools. You can construct a chart using MS Excel or a similar spreadsheet. Every activity has a separate line and you can schedule review and break points. You can move the time blocks around to report on actuals versus planned, and to re-schedule, and to create new plan updates. An example of a Gantt chart is given at the end of Chapter 3 on making a business case for ERM, page 53.

The purpose of the *issues log* is to be a summary of all the issues that the project might throw up, how they should be addressed, who is responsible for addressing them and their status (whether they are still open, resolved or passed on). The log is an extremely effective device for ensuring that all project issues are dealt with. It should be a principal item on the agenda for project board meetings. An example of a log is shown on page 54.

The *risk log* is designed to list all the identified risks in the project and to record the results of their evaluation and analysis. The resulting details are then managed as part of the process of delivering the planned benefits of the project. Each identified risk should be numbered and allocated an owner; an assessment should be made of its probability, impact and proximity (normally on a scale of 1 to 3 where 1 is low); and counter-measures and contingency plans drawn up. The purpose of the risk log is as a management tool to identify, analyse and 'manage down' risks to acceptable levels. An example of a risk log is shown on page 53.

A further important element of managing the progress of the project is change control. As issues and risks are identified and managed, there are very likely to be changes in project activities. Change control should be a formal process to ensure that changes and modifications are made in line with what has been identified and that any subsequent or related changes are managed effectively. When a formal request is made for something to be changed, it should be approved by the project board and recorded by the project manager. He/she should assess what impact is likely if the change is made (principally what cost might fall upon the project) and make plans for it to be implemented. The project board might wish to review the change again in the light of the results of this assessment and planning. After that the change can be made, tested and implemented.

Closing the project

When the new system has been tested, piloted and rolled out to the organization, a formal project closure report should be made by the project manager and submitted to the project board for approval. This report will need to be preceded by several undertakings, the outcome of which should be reflected in the report.

These will include:

- feedback from users on such issues as ease of use of the system, efficacy of the file plan, ability to find information as and when required, etc. – in short, those user-related benefits that were identified in the original business case
- an assessment of how well the project met time, cost and resource constraints
- lessons that can be learnt from the project
- the amount of training on the new system that was necessary and any ongoing support that needs to be given to users
- identification of any follow-on issues (for example, likelihood of upgrades to the software; performance of contractors)
- archiving and disposal of project documentation.

The original business case should be revisited to see how well anticipated benefits were realized. Given the length of a project of this kind, it ought to be expected that there will have been some changes in the working or other environments that may have negated some of the anticipated benefits.

References

Although the above sample is based on PRINCE 2 methodology, there are several other methodologies available. Among the more useful are the following:

The *Department of Education and Skills* provides a very straightforward methodology, well structured and with many links to detailed advice and guidance. www.dfes.gov.uk/ppm/index.cfm.

The *MindTools* website, as the name suggests, provides several management tools for undertaking projects. While they do not form a complete methodology in themselves, they can be put together in different combinations to form an effective way to manage your project. www.mindtools.com/pages/main/newMN_PPM.htm.

The *businessballs* website takes a very commonsense approach to project management. It is aimed at the private sector and splits the methodology into manageable chunks. www.businessballs.com/project.htm.

APPENDIX

Sample route map for implementing electronic records management

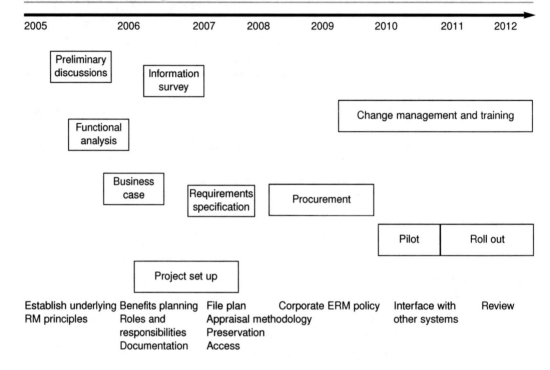

| 2005 | 2006 | 2007 | 2008 | 2009 | 2010 | 2011 | 2012 |

Preliminary discussions

Information survey

Change management and training

Functional analysis

Business case

Requirements specification

Procurement

Pilot

Roll out

Project set up

| Establish underlying RM principles | Benefits planning Roles and responsibilities Documentation | File plan Appraisal methodology Preservation Access | Corporate ERM policy | Interface with other systems | Review |

12

Procurement

It is very likely that you will have a specialist procurement function in your organization and that you will be required to follow set procedures. The following pages are an attempt to describe some context to the activity, what to bear in mind when undertaking the procurement of such a major item as an electronic records management system and to point to the experience of other organizations that can be utilized. They also set out the kinds of questions you might ask suppliers of systems and examine the role that testing might play in the procurement process.

Procurement procedures

The acquisition of an electronic records management system would be described as indirect procurement in that it concerns the purchase of operating resources to enable an organization to undertake its functions. 'Direct procurement' is the term more often used for the purchase of items that are part of finished products (raw materials, parts, etc.) and is more common in manufacturing settings.

For such a large acquisition as an electronic records management system, procurement will certainly involve a bidding process. This will involve a number of specific steps:

1 *business case* (see Chapter 3)
2 *requirements* – see Part 2; see also reference to the requirements catalogue on page 174
3 *specification* – often defined as 'a statement of needs to be satisfied by the procurement of external resources' and sometimes known as the 'statement of requirement' or 'operational requirement'. The purpose of the specification is to present prospective suppliers with a clear and accurate description of the organization's needs so that they can put forward their solution/proposal. The

specification is likely to be drafted by the project team and signed off by the senior responsible officer (see roles and responsibilities in Chapter 11). It ought to be reviewed by a member or members of the project board to ensure that it is complete and accurate. Key points to consider in this review are:

— the document is compatible with the business case

— requirements are complete, accurate and unambiguous

— the requirement is deliverable

— issues and risks have been properly addressed

— stakeholders' views have been taken into account

— future developments, including any business changes, have been taken into account.

A sample framework for a specification is shown at the end of this chapter. The requirements in the specification become part of the contract that is let to the successful supplier. Negotiations with prospective suppliers (see below) may lead to amendments to some of the requirements; this, however, should be handled with care to ensure that all suppliers receive fair and equal treatment. A practical issue may be the amount of background material that should be made available to prospective suppliers; as far as possible this should be in electronic form or, if this is not possible, a small library of material that suppliers can visit should be set up.

4 A large procurement like this will mean that an *advertisement* (to obtain expressions of interest) should be placed in the *Official Journal of the European Union* (OJEU). From time to time the European Union sets contract values above which threshold EU procurement provisions must be followed. At the time of writing the value for service and supply contracts was £154,000. See the website www.ogc.gov.uk/documentation_and_templates_ojeu_advertisement.asp.

5 An *evaluation plan* needs to be drawn up. What criteria will you use to assess the suitability of products and suppliers? Suggested areas for questions are given at the end of this chapter; these may need to be supplemented by key technical questions, which is where you will need to call in IT specialists. You will need to decide who will conduct the evaluation; the most suitable people will probably be the project board members. You will also need to decide what scoring system you will want to use for answers to the agreed questions. A simple system like that shown in Table 12.1 should be adequate.

6 A short-list of suppliers should then be drawn up based on an agreed 'pass mark' from the evaluation.

7 The resulting prospective suppliers should then be invited to give a presentation on their proposal. This will give you an opportunity to meet them and gain a better understanding of their approach. The presentation, and demonstration of the product, should be given to representatives from across the organization as well as to the project board members. The representatives should come from the main business areas affected. A similar set of questions to those used during the main evaluation can be compiled for the audience to mark, but they will need to

concentrate more on use of the system rather than the supplier's ability to provide it.

8 The project board will then need to evaluate all the questionnaire results and make the selection of the most suitable provider. It should be prepared for feedback requests from unsuccessful tenderers and, in this respect, should ensure that there is adequate documentation and an audit trail of decisions and actions.

Table 12.1 Evaluation scoring system

Score	Interpretation
–	The marker does not feel competent to make a judgement or requires more information
0	It will not meet our needs
1	There is considerable doubt as to whether it will meet our needs
2	A workable solution could be implemented
3	Confident that a solution to the requirement can be fully implemented
4	Outstanding response. The supplier exceeds the expectations set out in the invitation to tender, providing added value

System availability

Over the past ten years many electronic records management systems have been produced by many different companies. The market has expanded rapidly as policies in both public and private sectors have edged towards the management of records and information electronically. The great difficulty for most organizations, even after compiling business cases, undertaking records surveys, developing file plans and drawing up requirements, is to decide which will best suit their needs. Apart from the numerous systems available, you will have seen that the choice can be affected by the size of the organization, its approach to technology (centralized, decentralized, etc.), existing technology infrastructure and available skills.

To a certain extent you will be manoeuvred towards choosing a system from those companies who have expressed an interest as part of the procurement process. This, however, should not preclude you from examining different systems to assess their capability. You may even want to test some of them and most companies are more than happy to provide you with that opportunity. Testing and gaining experience with different systems is something you can do in the early stages, perhaps during the business case phase or as part of the gathering of requirements. A lot of work has already been done for you.

In the UK The National Archives drew up functional requirements for ERM systems in 1999 and embarked upon a testing programme of available systems. They subsequently produced a list of systems that demonstrated, in testing conducted by The National Archives, the capability to meet the functional requirements. Approval lasted for two years. When the functional requirements were revised in

October 2002, a new testing programme was undertaken and a similar list of approved systems was compiled. Detailed information about the testing programme, which came to a stop in 2005 in favour of, among other things, formal contribution to the development of MoReq (see page 42), is still available on The National Archives website: www.nationalarchives.gov.uk/electronicrecords/function.htm.

Common pitfalls

There are typical problems that befall organizations when undertaking major procurements such as this:

1 *Insufficient vendor or technology education* – the electronic records management systems market is large and crowded. There are many good systems but each supplier will have its own features and functions for its product that other suppliers do not have. Time investigating the market is time well invested; it will ease the process of writing requirements and evaluating proposals.

2 *Poorly defined requirements* – not enough time may be spent on understanding and documenting internal requirements with the result that they are so broadly stated as to be meaningless to a potential supplier. There may also be a danger that too many assumptions are made: most suppliers will have little or no knowledge of the organization's core business and some of the requirements may need to be spelt out in detailed but simple terms. For example, if a requirement is stated that the electronic records management system should support output to different formats including any future formats that may be developed, it invites suppliers to say one of two things:
   — they cannot support unknown formats (most, however, will not say that)
   — they will support future formats (which may not be true).

3 *Lack of consideration of key players* – users are often not given enough consideration when designing and implementing an electronic records management system. They are key to ensuring the success of the project at all its stages.

4 *Providing requirements that differ from one section to another* – a common mistake is not checking for consistency. For example, it might say in one section that the system should cater for 400 users but quote a different figure in another section.

5 *Insufficient budget* – researching systems and investigating the market will help to obtain a realistic budget for the project. There may be a danger, for example, of basing figures on out-of-date data. The time taken to develop and implement a system is often underestimated. In 1999 it was optimistically suggested that ERM systems could be introduced in UK government departments within five years. Experience has shown that this is more likely to take between seven and ten years.

6 *Insufficient time to complete key stages* – with the pressure of financial and other

restraints, project members are often not given enough time to complete business cases, specifications, file plans or other essential documents. Cutting corners with key documentation like this will cause problems for the end product.

APPENDIX
Framework for a specification

NB This specification is intended as a guide only. A procurement specification should reflect your organization's requirements and the particular circumstances of the procurement.

Introduction

• Background information on your organization
• The purpose and composition of the specification
• Any caveats or disclaimers.

Scope

• What will be included and excluded
• What is optional (proposals may be considered for extra facilities).

Background

• Current records management policies and procedures
• Functions
• Organization and staffing
• Stakeholders
• Workflow
• How the electronic records management procurement fits into the organization's overall IT/business strategy
• Procurement objectives
• Future developments in records and information management in the organization.

Requirements

• These should be classified as mandatory, highly desirable or desirable.
• These terms are often articulated by the words 'must', 'should' and 'may' respectively.
• There may also be some requirements that simply request information from potential suppliers.

Constraints

There may be some requirements that could constrain the solution put forward by prospective suppliers (for example, time constraints or the need to interface with existing IT packages, such as e-mail).

Implementation

- What methodologies will suppliers be using?
- What processes will suppliers use to implement solutions (for example, managing risk, project management)?

General contract conditions

These should include roles and responsibilities of key personnel.

Procurement procedures

- Timetable – although it should be made clear that events may cause this to change
- Evaluation criteria to be used
- Contacts in your organization from whom further information can be obtained.

Format and content of responses

How suppliers will be expected to respond to the specification.

Suggested question areas for an evaluation of proposals

Capability and experience

- Does the supplier's staff have the skills and experience to meet the requirements?
- Does the supplier's organization include relevant roles and responsibilities to manage the requirements?
- Has the supplier undertaken a project of similar type, scale and complexity before?
- How well does the supplier's experience and track record support their proposal (in, for example, customer relationships; successfully completed projects)?

Capacity

- Does the supplier have adequate resources to carry out the project (including numbers of experienced staff)?

- What other contracts does the supplier currently have active or is bidding for?
- Does the supplier provide adequate evidence of flexibility?
- Does the supplier provide evidence of the use of service level agreements for availability, and does it monitor performance in this respect?

Shared strategic aims

- How does your organization's specification fit with the supplier's core business (an indication of how important the contract might be to the supplier)?
- Are your organization's strategic aims compatible with those of the supplier?

Culture

- Is the supplier's culture compatible with your organization?
- Is there evidence that the supplier is committed to key values, personal development and culture change?
- Are the supplier's managers committed to business development and a strong organizational culture?

Organization and management

- What evidence is there of the effectiveness of the supplier's management in respect of financial, quality, performance, risk and change management?
- Does the supplier use a standard project management methodology?
- How does the supplier respond to new and changing customer requirements?
- Does the supplier have an appropriate performance management system?
- Is the supplier's financial management system capable of providing your organization with relevant information?
- Does the supplier use a particular customer relations management system?
- Does the supplier use a particular quality management system?
- What quality and management standards does the supplier use for benchmarking?
- Does the supplier have adequate support systems in place to undertake the contract (for example, documentation, records management systems)?
- Does the supplier have adequate contingency and business continuity plans in place?

Understanding

- Does the supplier's proposal demonstrate an understanding of the specification, in particular the requirements?
- Does the supplier understand the benefits that your organization is seeking from the project?

- Does the supplier demonstrate an understanding of the technical solutions it is proposing?
- Does the supplier understand your organization's core business?

Service provision

- Does the proposal include ongoing support and maintenance services for hardware and software?
- Does the proposal include provision of operational documentation for users? Is there evidence that the supplier has an effective change management system?
- Does the supplier demonstrate a positive attitude towards change?
- Are the supplier's proposals for service management adequate (resources, performance, service continuity, charging, reporting, feedback, dealing with incidents, etc.)?
- Does the supplier subscribe to any standards to support service provision?
- Does the supplier document service provision performance levels?
- How does the supplier propose to act upon customer feedback?
- Does the proposal include suggestions for a helpdesk facility?
- Does the supplier have adequate plans to show that key resources can be made available to meet customer needs?
- Is the supplier ready to take on and manage the risks associated with the specification and does its proposal include costs for taking on specified risks?
- Will the supplier use sub-contractors? If so, how will these be managed?
- Does the proposal define a recommended method of training on the proposed system?
- Does the proposal encompass security aspects, including arrangements for backing up?
- Does the proposal detail relevant product licence agreements?

Other

- Is the supplier committed to communication and the principle of an open working relationship built on trust?
- Will your organization be able to build a good working relationship with the supplier's project team?
- Will the supplier accommodate visits to their premises?

13

Change management

This chapter considers the changes that will need to be managed when implementing the electronic records management system. It revisits the subject of benefits and examines how they can be realized. Change management is itself a separate discipline and has a far wider application than we are considering here. Nevertheless, there are some important aspects of it that we should be aware of.

What do we need to change?

Electronic records management projects inevitably involve various changes in organizational responsibilities, policies and procedures. The capacity to manage these changes will determine the success of the implementation process. There are two main ways of promoting the acceptance of change – communication and training. First, however, in the context of electronic records management, there are still deep-seated traditions in the way we handle and provide information. There are three areas where these need to change.

Secrecy to openness

Over the past few years new openness initiatives in many areas have presented a major change in attitudes. For example, in the UK there were codes of practice on openness in the public sector from the 1990s. The White Paper *Open Government* – published in July 1993 – set out proposals for new legislation and for a code of practice on Access to Government Information. In subsequent years similar codes of practice were introduced for the Welsh Assembly, Scottish Executive and the National Health Service. These codes of practice all had the same basic premise – that people have access to available information about services provided, the cost of those services, quality standards and performance against targets; that they are provided with explanations about proposed changes and have an opportunity to influence decisions on such changes; and that they know what information is available and where they can get it. The Freedom of Information Act 2000 has now superseded all these codes. A culture of openness continues to seep through society, albeit slowly. People still keep information to themselves, however (perhaps they feel more powerful if they do so). They often query why anyone should need to know what they know. The change – and the challenge – is to recognize that we need to move away from the Need to Know towards the Right to Know.

Individual to corporate

Records management has long been considered a low priority for most organizations. Paradoxically, while the last decade or so has seen a greater emphasis on corporate planning and corporate targets, the supporting records and information sources have remained set along traditional lines. In a paper environment records were often centralized, but managers and operational staff needed live records to hand and often needed them immediately. In addition, the low-grade staff manning the perceived low-grade work in registries and record centres meant that many staff did not believe that they would ever see their files again if they put them away in the file store. When computers were introduced into the office environment those live records were increasingly stored on individual hard disks. When local area networks were introduced it seemed natural to maintain those folders that had been created, or at least duplicate them on the network. The concept of sharing information is struggling to emerge from these traditional attitudes. It is only in recent years, with the *Modernising Government* agenda and the greater availability of systems designed specifically to manage records corporately, that the change in culture is quickening. The attitude of 'my records in my cabinet in my office' (or even 'my records on my floppy disks') is no longer valid. Records and information created by individuals in the course of their official employment are corporate records and information and, with few exceptions, should be made available to the corporate body.

Paper to electronic

Until electronic records management systems are implemented, information systems in organizations will not always generate electronic records that fall under any formal corporate control and management. Local area networks are not capable of preventing the personal control of information. There are still many people who do not trust electronic records – but this is not something that will be overcome with the age generations; it has to be taken on board now if we are to meet our business targets, discharge our legal obligations and implement systems effectively. There are two examples that might illustrate this point:

1 Destruction of records – some organizations still insist on having written (and

signed) certification when records are destroyed. Why was this laid down in the first place? – to prove that destruction had taken place and had been undertaken by an authorized person. An electronic communication, perhaps in the form of an e-mail, will do just as well. Electronic audit systems can prove – probably more conclusively – that that e-mail was sent and sent by the person it says sent it.

2 There is still a misconception that e-mail messages are an ephemeral form of communication, but they are increasingly becoming the primary business tool for both internal and external working. The types of e-mail that might need to be managed as a record include discussions, information distributed to groups of people, agreement to proceed, and other exchanges relating to the discharge of business. E-mail messages can provide evidence about why a particular course of action was followed, which means that it is necessary not just to capture the e-mail relating to the final decision but also the discussions that might indicate why one decision was made as opposed to another. This is certainly important in a business context but may also be vital, for example, in answering freedom of information requests. As soon as an e-mail message needs to be forwarded for information purposes, it should be considered as a record. Furthermore, as soon as an e-mail message has been identified as a record of a business transaction, it is important that the message is retained with other records relating to that particular business activity.

Promoting the acceptance of change

A lot has been written about change management, and numerous management consultants and gurus have propounded several models. At the heart of the process, however, are people. The critical issue is that change deals with people: real people, with hopes, fears, needs and aspirations. We need to take into account the fact that they are very likely to interpret situations and opportunities through the filter of their own experiences and aspirations. Change is not a selling process. It needs to be understood and managed in such a way that people can cope effectively with it. Since it is an unsettling process, those managing the change need to be a settling influence. Management/leadership style and behaviour are more important than the adoption of a complicated process or model. People and teams need to be empowered to find their own solutions and responses, with facilitation and support from managers.

When planning to manage change there are *five* key principles to bear in mind:

1 different people react differently to change
2 everyone has fundamental needs that have to be met
3 change usually involves a loss of something
4 fears have to be dealt with
5 expectations need to be managed.

You may find the change management toolkit on the following website useful:

www.idea.gov.uk/idk/aio/6056931.

Communication

Since the implementation of an electronic records management system will affect a lot of people, use should be made of the communication strategy suggested in Chapter 11 (Project Management). Use it to ensure that information about organizational change is disseminated effectively and comprehensively. There is nothing worse than letting the grapevine take over in these kinds of situations. Give people time to express their views and respond to requests for information. Try to provide coaching or counselling to address their concerns. Be wary of using language like 'changing peoples' mindsets' or 'changing attitudes'. Expressions like this are usually indicative of an imposed or forced change. They also imply that the staff have the wrong mindset, which is often the responsibility of the organization itself, not the staff.

Apart from face-to-face communication (by far the best way of promoting the acceptance of change), you might consider holding workshops on implementation: they can be a very effective way of developing collective understanding and commitment to new procedures. Staff surveys are also a good way of gathering and measuring peoples' concerns so that they can be addressed directly as part of the change-management process. Finally, don't forget all the obvious means of communication – your organization's intranet, addressing departmental meetings, newsletters and perhaps a question & answer paper (which could follow on from information gathered from a survey).

Training

Training on use of the electronic records management system itself is examined in detail in the next chapter. As far as change management is concerned, it may be useful to set out the skills and strategies that might be used to achieve an effective change process.

People skills

This area includes communication and interpersonal skills, and, as we have already observed, managing change is predominantly about people. In taking into account user perception and expectations when implementing electronic records management, a major achievement will be to put ourselves in their place. We should try to see the situation through their eyes.

Political skills

It is probably stating the obvious that all organizations are very political. Managers of change are unlikely to be able to do much about this but they ought to be very aware of the situation they are facing. In addition, they have to make their own judgements and not give opinions in this respect.

Analytical skills

It will not be enough to make assumptions or guesses about the organization. Change managers need skills that will enable them to analyse systems and, in managing the progress of implementation, to analyse financial procedures in order to ensure that the project will come home on budget. In-depth analysis will produce conclusions that are difficult to argue against and will smooth the passage of implementation.

Business skills

This may be the easiest skill to acquire. The change manager must know the business of the organization. This is not just its core business but all those support functions that often get taken for granted.

System skills

The change manager must be familiar with electronic records management systems. This does not mean that he/she needs to be technically minded and understand the internal workings of hardware and software systems. There are usually plenty of IT experts to call upon for that. What is required here is an appreciation of the procedural role of electronic records management, how it fits in with records and information management generally and how it relates to the wider world of electronic ways of working (websites, intranets, etc.). An understanding of the underlying principles of records management set out in Chapter 1 is essential.

Change control

Change management can also refer to changes in the electronic records management software as it is tested, piloted or rolled out. A typical scenario would be a formal change request to a supplier/contractor (perhaps resulting from testing or from an issue that has arisen during project board discussions), who would then consider the technical and economical feasibility of implementing the change, and put forward a change proposal to the project manager. Depending on the nature and size of the change (particularly the cost), this will be agreed and signed off, and then implemented. Whatever the details of changes like this, they obviously need to be documented. A simple spreadsheet with the following headings is usually sufficient:

- change request number
- initiator
- date raised

- change request description
- allocated to
- priority
- response/comments
- current status.

Realization of benefits

As we saw in Chapter 3, identifying the benefits of introducing an electronic records management system is crucial to the development of the business case. Just as important, we cannot get away from the need to realize those benefits.

The management and realization of benefits need to be supported by the organization's strategic and business planning process. This will almost certainly use some system of performance indicators to measure business targets. The same should be adopted for measuring benefits from implementing the electronic records management system. There is the added point, of course, that this kind of integration of performance measurement gives the new system a high profile. We saw in Chapter 3 how benefits might be identified and categorized. In order for them to be measured we need to establish baselines for each indicator. For example, if we are going to measure the time taken to retrieve a document, we need to measure this prior to the electronic records management system being implemented. In this instance (and in similar categories) the baseline might comprise a measurement relating to a paper system and a measurement relating to electronic records stored on local area networks. In both cases it will be useful to measure the improvements that the new system will almost certainly generate. It is a good idea to establish the baseline measurements well before the electronic records management system is rolled out. By definition they cannot be drawn up after that stage, so it is as well not to leave them until the last minute. A good time to do them would be during the workshops set up as part of the identification phase of benefits management (see page 44).

Below are examples of the measurements that might be taken:

- volumes of records filed in the ERM system
- percentage of users filing records into the system
- percentage of records available to anyone in the organization (an indicator of how much information is being shared)
- percentage of users regularly retrieving records from the system
- percentage of records actually found on the system by users
- number of people who have received training.

The register of benefits (see Chapter 3) can be used to record the required measurements. However, it might also be useful to obtain at a specific time after roll-out the views of users by undertaking a survey or holding departmental workshops. This would supplement the statistics from the benefits register by indicating how the electronic records management system is contributing to individuals' abilities to undertake their duties, whether it improves their motivation and whether they are obtaining more or less job satisfaction – in other words, the qualitative benefits as well as the quantitative benefits. In addition, the survey could serve to show that the views of users are being given the highest priority as part of the change-management process. The kinds of questions you might ask in such a survey are shown in Figure 13.1.

The timing for undertaking such a survey will depend on local circumstances but it is common to allow at least ten weeks to elapse after roll-out before doing so.

Pattern of use
How long have you been using the ERM system?
Do you access the system remotely?
How do you rank yourself as a user? (accomplished, comfortable, reluctant, hesitant, non-user)
Why do you use/not use the ERM system?

Working methods
How many e-mails do you receive each day?
Do you file e-mails in the ERM system?
Do you file more or less than before the implementation of the ERM system?
Does your filing take more or less time than before the implementation of the ERM system?
Do you scan paper documents into the system?
Can you retrieve information now more or less easily than before the implementation of the ERM system?
What impact has the ERM system had on the way you work?

Views on the system
What are the two best functions of the ERM system?
What are the two worst functions of the ERM system?
What do you think of the appearance, design, etc. of the ERM system?
Which areas of the ERM system do you think you need to know more about?

Support
Does your management team encourage use of the ERM system?
Who would you contact first if you had a problem with the ERM system?
How often have you used the IT Helpdesk to solve a system problem?
If you have raised a problem with the ERM system:
Was it resolved satisfactorily?
Was the speed of response satisfactory?

Any other comments

Figure 13.1 Sample ERM survey
With acknowledgements to the Department of Health

14

Training

Training is the last, but no less essential, step in implementing the electronic records management system. This short chapter examines the key elements of training, concentrating mainly on delivery approaches. It presumes that some basic training – on records management principles and practices – has already been undertaken.

Procedural/technical training

User training will need to be a mix of procedural training – how the file plan works, naming conventions, disposal scheduling, etc. – and technical training – how the system functions. These are normally best undertaken together; indeed, they are probably inseparable in that a procedural understanding needs to be achieved by using the new system. Training should occur while installation of the new system is taking place so that users can immediately apply what they have learnt as soon as the system goes live.

There will be a practical problem that needs addressing and which will affect the programme or schedule of training that you will want to draw up – the availability of computers. Part of this is also the optimum number of attendees that will make the training sessions effective and worthwhile. Taking both these points into consideration, ten has generally been shown to be the best number for face-to-face training sessions.

A timetable of training sessions should be drawn up so that participants know well in advance when they will be expected to undertake the requisite training.

Delivery methods

Delivery should consist of a package of face-to-face/hands-on training and the provision of user manuals. It is generally not possible to train staff in one way without the other. In particular, user manuals are essential for later reference as well as being useful for those members of staff who may take longer than others in grasping training points in the hands-on forum. They can be provided in paper form or made available on an organization's intranet. User manuals, while focusing on the technical operation of the electronic records management system, should not be too technical themselves. They need to be understood by the average user, who will not have had any detailed technical training on, for example, the maintenance of computers or the structure of metadata schemes. The best user manuals use a combination of straightforward language, diagrams and screenshots. An example of two pages from a user manual (for the introduction of an automated digital records transfer system) is shown in the Appendix at the end of this chapter.

Face-to-face training could be given in-house or you may want to make use of outside consultants. The suppliers of the system themselves will often be able to offer training packages. There are, of course, advantages and disadvantages with both approaches. In-house training can sometimes be slower but it can provide more awareness of job requirements and better future support. Outside training can be faster but provide a limited awareness of job requirements. A compromise approach is often made – organizations send records management staff for training by the supplier and then use them to train their users. In this way they are able to incorporate the job requirements, working culture and specialist requirements into the training.

Some electronic records management systems may come with computer-based training packages, such as interactive CDs. All of them will have a 'Help' facility among their menu items.

Levels of training

Training on the new electronic records management system should be pitched at three levels:

- senior managers – those responsible for corporate strategy and policy
- other users – including line managers
- records liaison staff.

Senior managers

As well as being trained on how the system works, senior staff need to acquire an understanding of the wider issues involved with the introduction of electronic records management systems or changes in access to information provisions so that they can take decisions on strategy and resources. With such a major change in operational activities, they also need to champion the system so that it will achieve better buy-in from the functional areas for which they are responsible. As far as their training is concerned, they need to be brought into the implementation process at an early stage. Many, if not all, of them will also have been involved in the design process although, strictly speaking, not in a training context. As we saw from a discussion of communication strategies, senior managers and other users should be kept informed of the progress of implementation. For the former, this might be effected by short presentations at management board meetings or similar gatherings. These presentations need not be formal and can be kept relatively short – 15 minutes is common. The important point is to keep the ERM implementation process firmly on the governance agenda. Support from senior management is vital if the project is to be successful.

Other users

If users of the new system do not have a general understanding of records management principles and practices, this situation must be addressed first. Without such awareness they are very unlikely to become enthusiastic users of the electronic records management system. All users need to be familiar with the file plan and aware of the importance of good filing practices (such as the use of naming conventions) so that information can be quickly retrieved. They need to know who to approach or where to look if they are uncertain of what to do in the area of records management. They need to be familiar with good records maintenance procedures, including disposal scheduling in an electronic environment and the use of e-mail systems. As discussed above, there is a distinction here between procedural training and technical training. All, of course, need to know what buttons to push to make the electronic records management system work for them. Technical training on ERM systems is often at two levels – a day for introduction and further separate days to become familiar with some of the less common or less used aspects of the new system. User manuals (see above) form an important part of the training package, especially on the technical side.

Records liaison staff

A vital aspect of the framework of records and information management in an organization is to establish and maintain a network of staff in the various business areas who have local responsibility for records. In very large organizations these staff might be full-time and be engaged in appraising and reviewing records in their business areas or be responsible for administering local file plans. More often than not, however, they will have other responsibilities. Such staff will not normally be under the direct command of the records manager.

As far as a new electronic records management system is concerned, the training of records liaison staff needs to be more detailed than that of their colleagues. They will be the focal point of operations when it comes to implementing the new system in their business areas and they will be able to deflect some of the more detailed or business-focused queries away from the records manager. They should not be expected, however, to deal with technical questions; there will still be a need to refer to IT specialists. Their training, therefore, should automatically include some of the lesser-used aspects of the system and will likely comprise three or four days.

Supplementary training materials

The face-to-face training and user manuals can be supplemented by leaflets, booklets and checklists, which can be an effective way of helping users to become familiar quickly with the common functions of the system. An example is shown in Figure 14.1.

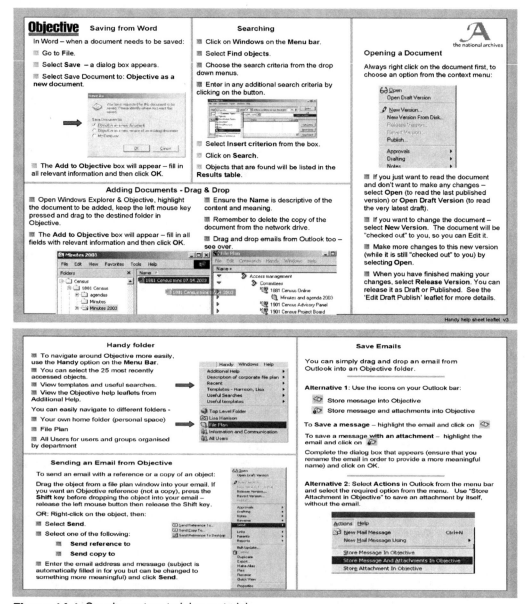

Figure 14.1 Supplementary training material
Reproduced with kind permission from The National Archives

APPENDIX
Sample pages from a user manual

(Reproduced with kind permission from The National Archives)

Creating a Follow-Up Accession (Record Management Executive)

If the OGD has Deliverable Units that were retained from a previous Accession, and they now want to transfer them to TNA, you must create a second (then third, fourth etc.) accession for the original Accumulation.

1 From the Create New Accession screen first (as for the first Accession) select the Department and Series to which the Accession applies. A list of previous Accumulations for the Series (if any have been created) will be listed.
2 Click on the original Accumulation. This can only be done if one or more Deliverable Units were indicated as 'Retained' from a previous Accession. A new screen should appear, as shown in Figure A14.1.

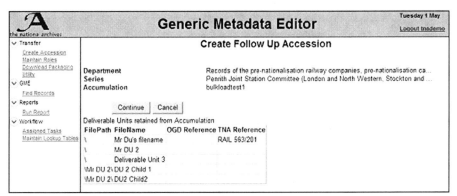

Figure A14.1 Create Follow-Up Accession
Reproduced with kind permission from The National Archives

3 Confirm your Accumulation choice by clicking the Create Accession button. (or click Back if you do not want to create another Accession for this Accumulation). This should take you to the Assign Roles screen (Figure A14.2).

Assigning Roles (Record Management Executive and Managers)

Whether you are creating a first or follow-up Accession for an Accumulation, the next step is to identify the individuals who will be involved in the process.

The assigned users can be changed at any time during the process by any role Manager, by selecting Transfer > Maintain Roles from the left-hand menu.

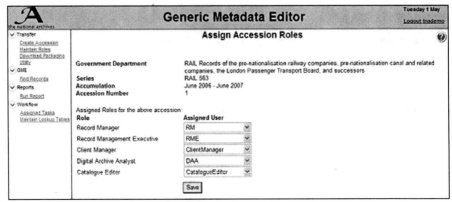

Figure A14.2 Assign Accession Roles
Reproduced with kind permission from The National Archives

If re-assigning users to roles during the Transfer Process, first select the required 'Government Department', 'Series', 'Accumulation' and 'Accession Number' in turn from the drop-down lists. The currently assigned individual to each role will be displayed. Then assign roles, as follows:

1 (Re)assign an individual to any role by selecting a user's name from the corresponding drop-down list. The RME (at least) should already be assigned, but they can be reassigned. You cannot leave any role unassigned.

If an expected user's name does not appear in one of the lists, please contact the Digital Preservation Department. All roles must be assigned to an individual. If you are not sure who should be assigned to a particular role please select the first role Manager in the list.

2 Click on the 'Save' button and wait for the confirmation message. This will sends e-mails to all the assigned users so they know that they will be involved later in the process. It will also send an e-mail to the OGD Record Manager to prompt them to perform the first task (Maintain Accession Metadata).

This completes the initiation of a new accession.

Part 4

The future

15

The future of information management

Records and information management is going through a period of huge change, not least because of the challenges posed by electronic records. In a wider context we are living in a rapidly changing world where there are now over one billion users of the internet and over 60% of electronic access to information is from mobile devices. The paradox is that electronic information is essentially ephemeral and, if we are going to adapt to this changing environment, we need to think seriously about the sustainability of this information.

The creators of information are no longer records management professionals. There is a perceived lack of expertise in the field. The interest and developmental efforts are towards the technology rather than its product. We should not be surprised at that, but we must engage with the technical experts to ensure that the needs of both information management and information technology practitioners are met.

The traditional view of records and information managers is just that – traditional. Let's acknowledge that we are beginning to adapt, but more needs to be done. There are what many people like to call paradigm shifts in most aspects of the management of records and information. For example, the creation of information involves a greater understanding of metadata. This was unheard of in the paper environment when such data (we usually called it 'documentation') was taken for granted as part of the structure of registry and filing systems. There were file lists and (if you were lucky) disposal schedules which generally provided the metadata that you needed. Any extra was written on the file covers of records. Metadata in the electronic environment, however, requires considerably more thought and attention. There are different electronic systems so there will be different metadata schemes. This means different metadata standards and a constantly evolving field of information management. Another huge change is in the area of the retention of information. Appraisal methodologies have needed to be developed to cope with the electronic environment. For example, we no longer have the luxury of being able to undertake a (relatively) relaxed examination of records that are twenty years or so old, at which stage we feel more comfortable and confident in making a decision on historical value. Nor can we detach a judgement on historical value from one of business value. Both need to be made before the electronic record is obsolete.

We have to acquire new skills and knowledge to handle records and information in this changing world. A comparison of a glossary of records terms as recently as twenty years ago with that in Chapter 2 of this book only serves to emphasize this need. We should not, however, get too carried away with this recognition. Some of the traditional values and skills of records management are as important as they were then. For example, we still need those analytical skills to develop structures for the creation of records; we still need those decision-making skills to make judgements on the retention of information; and we still need those influencing skills to persuade others of the value of good record and information management practices.

Users of information increasingly expect everything online, 24 hours a day, seven days a week – and they increasingly expect information to be instantly available. How often do you curse your computer for being slow in retrieving information when in reality it is taking only a few seconds to display a mass of information? However unreasonable we may think this to be, we have to meet these expectations and recognize them for what they are – part of the changing world in which we live.

What does all this mean for the information management profession? It means that we are moving from a predictable world of paper to a volatile world of all kinds of information. As such we need to manage this information more effectively to continue to meet expectations and maintain standards. We need to take urgent steps to ensure the preservation of electronic information. If we don't, we will lose it. Lastly, users will expect us to deliver and interpret information ever more quickly and ever more intelligently, and we need to be prepared for that.

Records and information management has never been more important for underpinning good business practice and for complying with the regulatory environment. More and more organizations in both public and private sectors are building large infrastructures to manage information. Typically they will comprise

- core components (visions, principles, policies, etc.)
- standards and guidance (including legislation)
- resources – for users and for information managers
- co-ordination and communication.

As information management is becoming more integrated – where content, context, structure, data quality and resource discovery work harmoniously together – we begin to think of it as knowledge. There are now initiatives to take forward new business models involving the creation and integration of knowledge. Who knows where all this will lead to? Lest you think that it will not happen, remember the person who (allegedly) said in 1993: 'The Internet? We are not interested in it.' That was Bill Gates.

Appendix
Competency framework

List of competencies
(Reproduced with kind permission from The National Archives)

Core Competencies:
- Knowledge and History of the Organization
- Knowledge of the [sectoral] Environment
- Professionalism
- Communication and Promoting Records Management
- Team Working
- Planning and Time Management
- IT Literacy
- Flexibility
- Customer Care/Client Focus.

Functional Competencies:
- Information Management
- Information Technology
- Information Policy
- Records Management and Archival Practice
- Administration
- Specialist Knowledge.

Managerial Competencies:
- Coaching and Development
- Influencing
- Manage Performance
- Maintaining Standards
- Manage People
- Manage Projects.

Core Competencies

Level	Description
Knowledge and history of the organization	
1	• Has a basic understanding of the function and role of the organization, both past and present, and can explain this to others • Is familiar with the structure of the organization
2	• Understands the remit afforded to the organization by legislation and regulation, both past and present • Understands the different record-keeping systems used by the organization over the past 25 years or more and can explain them to others • Is aware of the high-profile subjects covered by the organization and their implications on records work
3	• Understands and acts on implications of past and present processes in the organization, including the appraisal of records • Explains and advises on the changes in the organization's role and responsibilities over the past few years and the documentary evidence supporting them
4	• Visualizes the future role of records within the organization • Coaches colleagues in developing their knowledge and understanding of the organization both past and present
Knowledge of the business environment (Business used as an example of a particular sector)	
1	• Understands how the organization fits into the particular business sector
2	• Understands how the business policy processes work • Is aware of the implications of business policy on records work and can explain this to others • Demonstrates own knowledge of the particular business environment in decision making • Demonstrates a knowledge of business history
3	• Is able to identify records implications of new policy • Actively improves own understanding of the business and the decision-making process
4	• Understands changes in commercial structures and practices and analyses impact on the business • Is able to influence policy processes outside the business • Is seen by others as an expert source of advice on the business history • Coaches colleagues to generate greater insight into commercial roles and organizations
Professionalism	
1	• Creates a positive impression with customers and clients • Is delivery focused • Responds promptly to requests for advice • Refers difficult questions to experts and ensures that action is taken to resolve issues
2	• Provides objective professional advice to clients • Communicates records policy consistently to clients and colleagues • Has a confident approach in the application of records management • Seeks to maintain current level of expertise
3	• Demonstrates relevant expertise and applies this consistently in records work • Is up to date with developments in own field of expertise and applies this in own work • Takes ownership of client issues and ensures their successful resolution • Deals confidently with senior managers in other divisions

Continued on next page

Level	Description
4	• Initiates records policy • Informs records policy with best practice approach • Role models standards to colleagues
Communication and promoting records management	
1	• Is clear and precise in written and oral communication • Can make simple presentations • Makes best use of available means of communication
2	• Communicates effectively to different audiences • Generates interest and enthusiasm in others • Translates technical terms into formats appropriate for their audience
3	• Develops opportunities for raising the profile of records management • Produces effective communication and marketing plans • Can assimilate and disseminate complex information • Is able to interpret a brief, and create and deliver an effective presentation to large groups
4	• Is an effective and inspirational speaker • Is persuasive and influential when conversing with others • Enhances communication and marketing through the development and implementation of communication and marketing strategies
Team working	
1	• Provides support for colleagues on own initiative • Understands own and others' roles within the team • Recognizes the need for teamwork
2	• Energetically pursues team targets • Willingly undertakes different team roles • Forms good working relationships with other teams
3	• Builds team effectiveness • Sets and communicates direction for a team • Generates enthusiasm for team and individual goals
4	• Able to select team members according to business needs and individual development requirements • Role models team working • Identifies and manages the collective responsibility of the team • Aims to develop the team's collective ability
Planning and time management	
1	• Completes tasks allocated on time • Understands the requirement to manage the time resource • Prioritizes according to organizational policy • Manages conflicting priorities in own work
2	• Plans and manages own workload to ensure completion • Monitors progress against targets and takes corrective action when required • Accurately plans out activities according to workload requirements • Works methodically
3	• Ensures that resources within a project or task are best deployed to meet targets • Delegates tasks effectively to others and ensures that they have the skills to succeed • Uses past experience to inform project planning and work allocation • Resolves priority conflicts for team members

Continued on next page

Level	Description
4	• Allocates assignments in the most efficient way • Recognizes the importance of making personal time available for individual person management • Generates options to address resource issues • Is solutions focused
IT literacy	
1	• Demonstrates basic knowledge of relevant IT packages and systems * • Uses this knowledge to perform own work efficiently
2	• Demonstrates good knowledge of relevant IT packages and systems * • Actively seeks to extend competence in information systems
3	• Able to use relevant specialist software in the organization • Able to use records management software packages • Coaches colleagues in the use of software and hardware
4	• Identifies requirements for new, or new versions of, software applications • Maintains a good level of knowledge of IT developments • Advises colleagues on IT issues
* *Relevant IT packages and systems include word processing, spreadsheets, databases, e-mail and the internet.*	
Flexibility	
1	• Willing to accept changes to job content • Adapts personal schedule to meet critical demands and to support colleagues • Is responsive to client and/or client needs
2	• Moves willingly between different jobs • Works easily with different people • Displays ability to apply policy flexibly • Works effectively in a changing environment
3	• Initiates and manages change • Is professionally innovative • Shows ability to alter management style to suit different situations • Is results orientated
4	• Role models and encourages flexibility in others • Creates a flexible culture for others • Seeks to improve performance and the working environment through change and innovation
Customer care/client focus	
1	• Understands the importance of ongoing customer care • Adjusts personal style to deal with different customers • Recognizes the importance of service levels
2	• Builds relationships at a number of different levels in a customer's organization • Understands clients' needs • Has systematic contact with customers on a regular basis • Formulates and manages service-level agreements with customers
3	• Actively solicits feedback from customers • Ensures continuity of service levels through mentoring and coaching • Makes every effort to ensure that customers have the necessary resources to meet required records management standards • Monitors service levels for a number of customers and deals with conflicting demands • Provides expertise and coaches others in customer care

Continued on next page

Level	Description
4	• Develops policies for achieving close and effective relationships with customers • Actively develops relationships with customers at a senior level • Seeks and uses feedback from customers to improve customer care

Functional Competencies

Information management	
1	• Recognizes and understands the differences between various types of electronic records and the systems which produce them
2	• Is able to supervise the inventory and audit of electronic records assemblies • Is able to provide advice on the development and application of procedures for managing electronic records
3	• Advises colleagues on mapping the information flows between different systems, putting the information in a business context, and assesses the implications of new systems development on electronic and paper records • Actively encourages colleagues to use and manage records as information assets • Contributes to the development of corporate records policies
4	• Develops an understanding of information policy and its implications for electronic records • Develops and maintains outside contacts to keep abreast of information management issues and techniques • Generates new and innovative approaches to tackling information management issues

Information technology	
1	• Has a basic knowledge of software and hardware applications and their usage in the organization
2	• Has practical experience of software/systems design and the provision of ongoing support • Is able to generate solutions to ensure the continuing integrity of data held by the organization
3	• Is able to develop an IT strategy for records and to contribute to organization-wide IT strategies • Demonstrates an awareness of leading edge developments in IT • Is able to implement an electronic document management system • Understands the implications of related office systems, such as workflow and image processing, for records management systems • Liaises with relevant IT specialists in other sectors
4	• Generates approaches to electronic records management issues emerging from IT strategies • Challenges and develops others' knowledge of IT systems and developments

Information policy	
1	• Understands and can explain to others the implications of the organization's information policy • Continuously develops own understanding of the information policy
2	• Facilitates liaison with other information professionals • Demonstrates awareness of issues relating to the management of current information • Understands the implications of information legislation and can interpret and apply relevant guidelines
3	• Contributes to the development of responses to changes in information policy • Ensures that own reports understand changes in information policy
4	• Is consulted as an expert on information policy • Provides guidance and advice on the implications of Data Protection and similar legislation • Develops organizational information policy and expertise

Continued on next page

Level	Description
Records management and archival practice	
1	• Is aware of different records media and associated records management implications • Has a basic knowledge of document preservation • Demonstrates knowledge of packaging, transfer and storage techniques
2	• Is able to interpret and apply guidelines on the management of conventional and electronic records • Follows best-practice principles in managing records • Demonstrates knowledge of records legislation
3	• Seeks to think creatively about the records management and archival process • Has a knowledge of other records repositories and their specialisms • Applies records management standards and best-practice guidelines in storing, appraising and selecting appropriate records
4	• Develops records management policies which reflect best practice and legislative environment • Is seen as an expert on records management and archives administration within the organization and externally • Uses experience and knowledge to coach others in records management • Is involved with external bodies in the further development of best practice in records management and archives administration
Administration	
1	• Administers simple tasks successfully and learns from mistakes • Follows procedures • Able to use basic office equipment • Respects and maintains the confidential nature of records and information entrusted to them • Pays attention to detail
2	• Checks for accuracy in other people's work • Creates and administers simple budgets • Administers complex tasks successfully • Maintains an effective filing system • Works within agreed procedures
3	• Initiates invoices • Demonstrates a basic working knowledge of procurement and contract management • Works within and monitors procedures
4	• Allocates administrative tasks across team members • Monitors the administration of a number of complex tasks
Specialist knowledge (Specialist knowledge might include: understanding of statistical research and sampling techniques; knowledge of particular types of records; specialist IT knowledge)	
1	• Demonstrates a basic knowledge of the subject • Is able to access sources for more information/greater detail
2	• Demonstrates a good knowledge of subject, both in theory and application • Is able to apply knowledge to current working environment
3	• Demonstrates an in-depth subject knowledge • Provides relevant and helpful advice to others • Shares knowledge willingly
4	• Demonstrates a subject knowledge in breadth and depth • Is seen as an expert and consulted by others regularly

Continued on next page

Managerial Competencies

Level	Description
Coaching and development	
1	• Takes personal responsibility for own development • Continuously improves personal competence in line with requirements of own job and career aspiration • Regularly seeks feedback on personal performance
2	• Regularly discusses training and development needs with staff, linking them with individual and team business targets • Identifies and agrees training and development needs and ensures that they are met • Actively supports staff throughout the training process, by briefing and debriefing, and provides information about available training
3	• Identifies potential and expertise in others • Measures and evaluates impact of training and development initiatives • Ensures individuals' knowledge is shared and captured
4	• Creates and encourages a culture of knowledge sharing within the organization • Creates opportunities to enhance learning and knowledge across the organization • Identifies and implements career-development opportunities for staff
Influencing	
1	• Is able to identify the benefits of records management policies • Is assertive with others in ensuring understanding of key information • Understands and can apply own influencing styles
2	• Is able to describe to others the benefits of changing records management practices • Is able to utilize a range of persuasion techniques • Understands how to influence others • Recognizes when to be assertive to achieve results
3	• Is able to change existing records management behaviours • Is able to moderate personal style with others to maximize outcomes • Is able to create change in records management policies throughout the organization
4	• Facilitates inter-departmental debates on records management best practice • Coaches others in developing their influencing skills • Works to ensure that the records section is closely involved in the organizational decision-making process
Manage performance	
1	• Contributes to the achievement of individual and team targets • Monitors own performance on a regular basis
2	• Identifies potential risks to performance achievement and responds promptly • Sets clear and achievable team targets and objectives, and manages their successful achievement • Understands how processes underlie performance
3	• Uses resources to maximize cost effectiveness of service provision • Consistently delivers targets within budget and provides accurate management information • Is able to develop corporate and business plans with useful measures of performance
4	• Manages collective performance to achieve business priorities and objectives • Allocates and manages resources to ensure the achievement of business priorities and objectives • Manages risk in order to maintain performance levels • Encourages others to initiate change to improve performance

Continued on next page

Level	Description
Maintaining standards	
1	• Understands and communicates the need for quality standards • Able to identify and implement ideas for improved quality of service in own work • Consistently applies records management standards
2	• Implements changes to quality standards • Able to identify and implement ideas for improved quality of performance • Recognizes resource constraints in achieving quality standards
3	• Generates standards to meet organizational needs • Promotes quality improvement throughout the organization • Seeks feedback on overall quality of service • Monitors standards and provides management information as required
4	• Promotes quality improvements in records management • Creates a culture that promotes the need for standards • Ensures availability of accurate quality information for management reporting
Manage people	
1	• Manages self and others in the completion of a task • Represents the needs of colleagues to superiors • Understands the performance-management system and ensures that own contribution is valid • Demonstrates commitment to personal development
2	• Recognizes and rewards good performance both formally and informally • Reviews individual and team performance and provides feedback • Forms effective working relationships • Delegates effectively to others
3	• Creates and communicates direction in a clear and consistent way • Enhances productive working relationships • Consults and communicates with others in areas of joint interest • Provides effective change management
4	• Creates an environment in which people are motivated and inspired • Creates a culture where individuals and teams own the impact of their actions • Provides leadership and direction during change
Manage projects	
1	• Can plan and deliver simple projects • Monitors progress against objectives • Understands basic project management techniques
2	• Identifies project objectives, risks and success factors • Delivers projects according to time, cost and quality targets • Takes action where progress is not in line with objectives • Understands and can apply a range of project management techniques • Manages suppliers on a day-to-day basis
3	• Manages complex or multiple projects • Manages contracts with external suppliers • Identifies in advance potential risks and their solutions • Creates, develops and manages project teams • Is able to negotiate satisfactory contracts with suppliers
4	• Is seen by others as an expert in project management • Generates, communicates and maintains a best-practice project management model • Ensures deliverables are in line with business strategies

Example of a profile: records manager

Role: develop and manage an organization-wide records management programme designed to ensure that records practices are effectively meeting the organization's objectives

Competence	Level
Core	
Knowledge and History of the Organization	3
Knowledge of the [*sectoral*] Environment	3
Professionalism	3
Communication and Marketing	3
Team working	2
Planning and Time Management	3
IT Literacy	2
Flexibility	3
Customer Care/Client Focus	3
Score:	25
Functional	
Information Policy	3
Information Management	2
Information Technology	1
Records Management and Archival Practice	3
Administration	2
Specialist Knowledge	3
Score:	14
Managerial	
Coaching and Development	3
Influencing	3
Manage Performance	3
Maintaining Standards	3
Manage People	2
Manage Projects	3
Score:	17
Total score:	56

Index

Information Rights in Practice:
the non-legal professional's guide

Alan Stead

Overstretched professionals in every public authority are grappling with the chalkface implications of a raft of legislation relating to information use. This is the first book to offer a single point of reference and advice, which can be understood by the non-legal professional.

The requirements of the relevant legislation are set out together with examples, flow-charts, and diagrams to illustrate and clarify how to apply the law in practice. This indispensable guide is a one-stop shop for all you need to know about information rights law, using relevant case studies to clarify and illuminate these tricky issues. Contents include:

- Data Protection Act 1998: definitions of personal data; scope of the Act; the principles; access to personal data and data sharing
- Freedom of Information Act 2000 and the Environmental Information Regulations 2004: scope of the Acts; applications of exemptions/exceptions; public interest tests, publication schemes; disclosure logs and records management
- Regulation of Investigatory Powers Act 2000
- Human Rights Act 1998
- Reuse of Public Sector Information Regulations 2005
- other non-information rights-related legislation
- interaction of legislation
- requests for information.

A must-have for anyone working with information rights in public authorities and the private sector, this book is also a useful reference point for legal advisers, academics and students of information rights, as well as media professionals wanting to learn and understand how public authorities approach requests for information and the surrounding procedures.

Alan Stead is an experienced practitioner in information rights, having managed a team at a unitary authority, and now runs his own training organization. He is an external examiner in a LLM in Information Rights, chairs the National Association for Information Management and is a member of a number of government consultation groups.

November 2007; 192pp; paperback; ISBN 978-1-85604-620-6; £39.95

Understanding Data and Information Systems for Recordkeeping

Philip C. Bantin

Content management systems, data warehouses, relational databases – the ways an institution can organize and store its information are changing rapidly, and it can be difficult to make sense of the myriad options.

This timely book is a comprehensive guide to the new technologies that can help information professionals and records managers better organize vital documents and information for preservation, search, and retrieval.

Bantin looks at the major types of recordkeeping resources – relational databases; data warehouses; and content, document, and knowledge management systems – and the ways in which each captures, stores and manages records. Each system is evaluated in light of its ability to manage digital content over the long term. The book also offers suggestions for adapting turnkey systems to better serve organizational needs, tips for implementing systems assessment, and guidance for ensuring that systems comply with legal requirements.

The complex area of e-mail management is also covered.

This book is an essential resource for information professionals and records managers, and for any organization interested in utilizing technology to better maintain their organizational records and data.

Philip C. Bantin is Adjunct Associate Professor, School of Library and Information Science, and Director of Archives at Indiana University, USA.

2007; 200pp; paperback; ISBN 978-1-85604-627-5; £44.95